What's Faith Got to Do with It?

What's Faith Got to Do with It?

Learning to Love and Live the Questions

JOHN CLAYTON LENTZ JR.

WIPF & STOCK · Eugene, Oregon

WHAT'S FAITH GOT TO DO WITH IT?
Learning to Love and Live the Questions

Copyright © 2025 John Clayton Lentz Jr. All rights reserved. Except for brief quotations in critical publications or reviews, no part of this book may be reproduced in any manner without prior written permission from the publisher. Write: Permissions, Wipf and Stock Publishers, 199 W. 8th Ave., Suite 3, Eugene, OR 97401.

Wipf & Stock
An Imprint of Wipf and Stock Publishers
199 W. 8th Ave., Suite 3
Eugene, OR 97401

www.wipfandstock.com

PAPERBACK ISBN: 978-1-6667-8508-1
HARDCOVER ISBN: 978-1-6667-8509-8
EBOOK ISBN: 978-1-6667-8510-4

VERSION NUMBER 09/08/25

All Scripture quotations unless otherwise marked are from the COMMON ENGLISH BIBLE. © Copyright 2011. COMMON ENGLISH BIBLE. All rights reserved. Used by permission. (www.CommonEnglishBible.com).

Scripture quotations marked (NRSVUE) are taken from the New Revised Standard Version Updated Edition. Copyright © 2021 National Council of Churches of Christ in the United States of America. Used by permission. All rights reserved worldwide.

To my beloved Deanne, who always
encourages me to move beyond my comfort zone.

To my parents, Jack and Robbie,
my brothers Peter and Andrew,
for their nurturing support.

To Jack, Meg, and Sarah,
for putting up with me all these years!

Be patient toward all that is unsolved in your heart and try to love the questions themselves, like locked rooms and like books that are now written in a very foreign tongue. Do not now seek the answers, which cannot be given you because you would not be able to live them. And the point is, to live everything. Live the questions now. Perhaps you will then gradually, without noticing it, live along some distant day into the answer.

—RAINER MARIA RILKE, *LETTERS TO A YOUNG POET*

Accentuate my confusion
until I shed those grandiose expectations
that divert me from the small, glad gifts
of the now and the here and the me.

—TED LODER, *"PRY ME OFF DEAD CENTER"*

Contents

Acknowledgments | ix
Introduction | xi

Chapter 1: Taking the Questions Seriously | 1
Chapter 2: James, Madelaine, and the Group | 11
Chapter 3: Loving the Questions | 22
Chapter 4: Mapping the Journey | 27
Chapter 5: God? | 32
Chapter 6: Who Is Jesus? | 45
Chapter 7: What Is the Bible and How Do You Read It? | 66
Chapter 8: Is Christianity the Only Way to the Mountaintop? | 80
Chapter 9: Can Christians Be Political Without Being Right Wing? | 91
Chapter 10: How Do I Pray? | 104
Chapter 11: What About Sex and the Bro Culture? | 113
Chapter 12: Do I Have to Believe in the Virgin Birth? Creeds and Confessions | 123
Chapter 13: What Do I Have to Believe? Conclusion | 129

Selected Bibliography | 135

Acknowledgments

THIS BOOK IS THE result of many years of formation. I could not have done it alone. I thank Jill Roberts for asking me, "What do I have to believe to be a Christian?" Friends Mark Joseph, Karen Long, and Graham Creasy encouraged me to put fingers to keyboard and share my thoughts. Amy Wheatley, the director of Christian education at the Forest Hill Church, Presbyterian, in Cleveland Heights, Ohio, organized the meeting of the young adult new members of the church to have a conversation. To Jake and Em, Kathryn and Scott, Dee Dee and Kurt, Sheryl, Isaac, Beatrice, Margaret—thank you for sharing your deepest thoughts with such clarity and honesty. I give thanks for the support and nurture of the Forest Hill Church congregation. They formed me into the Christian I am. It was an honor and privilege to serve them as their pastor for thirty years.

A January at Ghost Ranch in Abiquiu, New Mexico, gave me the time and space to write, wander, and wonder. To Jack, Meg and Sarah, Grant, and Jordan for putting up with my questions. To Professor Amos N. Guiora who is doing crucially important work on sexual abuse in organizations and institutions, including the church. He always remembers me in his books, so I am remembering him in mine. Finally, this book would not have been possible without the help and friendship of Dr. William "Chief" Meyer, who introduced me to Matthew Wimer at Wipf and Stock Publishers.

Introduction

THIS BOOK IS WRITTEN for those for are interested in knowing more about Christianity but for whom traditional pat answers don't satisfy. This book is for those who are curious about life and what really matters. It is for those who want their questions to be taken seriously. This book is for those who have been hurt by the church—told that they didn't belong or that God didn't love them as they are. It is for those who love the questions, seeking meaning and purpose for their lives.

I want to reframe the answers to the questions that I have been asked and that I too have struggled with. I still believe that Christianity is a way of living in this world that is transformative, powerful, and good. Christianity still has a place in the public arena and at tables of discussion and decision-making. I want to engage with the new generation of seekers, inviting them to pay attention to their questions.

Over the years I found myself discarding the old religious language, the doctrines and the dogmas that were no longer life-giving to me. I loved the study of Scripture, the preaching/hearing of a good sermon, the practices of spiritual disciplines, the joy of a fellowship dinner, the humbling experiences of being present at life-changing events, and getting involved in political social action that seemed to me to be a biblical imperative. I wanted to be a follower of Jesus, but I wasn't sure I believed all the other "stuff." The experiences, actions, and practices became more important

Introduction

to me than belief statements. Furthermore, I had learned so much from other faith traditions and spiritual practices. Why couldn't the differences be honored and the similarities be celebrated? Why did one have to be better, or right, and the others wrong?

Like so many others, I had more questions than answers. It wasn't that I became a doubter—that I didn't believe anymore—it was more that all this religious talk was dissatisfying. I felt the urge to break it all down and start over. Hence, the current project.

The questions that drive this book, the questions I want to "love," "live," and circle around, came from three main sources:

1. questions that I have been asked by church members, friends, skeptics, and cynics throughout my years in ministry;
2. questions raised at a study group conversation with a dozen individuals who mostly fit in the forty and under demographic; and
3. questions I myself have wrestled with for decades.

Why is this book important? We are living in a time of disruption. The old coalitions are not holding. The usual ways of speaking about politics, culture, religion have changed. The traditional orthodoxies are not only being questioned, they are being thrown out. Competing voices and messages overwhelm us—dividing us into tribes. Institutions are no longer trusted. Skepticism has changed into cynicism. A narrow Christian orthodoxy has become a weaponized force to divide and conquer.

However, times of disruption are also times of opportunity to rethink, reclaim, and restore. In the pages that follow, I will seek to reframe and answer some of the questions that people have raised about Jesus, religions, sex, and belief. However, I do not presume to be an answer man or give a definitive and final response to any of them. In fact, I want the reader to join me in "thinking aloud." If my attempts at reconstruction don't work for you, find your own answers that make sense. This is not a right or wrong process. Rather, it is an invitation to a journey. I want to invite you to find your way to a new revelation in these days of disruption.

INTRODUCTION

In the pages that follow, I invite seekers, doubters, and skeptics to explore issues of Christian belief. I will offer my thoughts about how to frame some answers to the questions, but my hope is to expand possible meanings. I want to celebrate the confusion and enjoy the wandering and wondering journey. Together, perhaps we can affirm some of the mystery, unpack some of the confusion, and celebrate the exciting task of putting words to what our guts feel—and our hearts yearn for.

CHAPTER 1

Taking the Questions Seriously

AFTER READING A RECENT report from the Pew Research Center,[1] several things caught my attention. Since 2007 there has been a sixteen-point decline in the number of US adults who identify as Christian. Furthermore, there has been a 25 percent decline in the share of self-described political liberals who identify as Christian since 2007. Religiously unaffiliated adults—meaning those who identify as atheists, agnostics, or as "nothing in particular"—account for 29 percent of the population. Yet, 86 percent of the respondents shared that they are spiritual or have a "supernatural outlook on the world." Eighty-three percent believe in God or a universal spirit. Seventy-nine percent believe that there is something spiritual beyond the natural world, and 70 percent believe in an afterlife. The report indicated that younger Americans (eighteen to twenty-four years of age) remain far less religious than older adults, with only 46 percent identifying as Christian and 43 percent identifying as religiously unaffiliated. As with older adults, younger adults who identify as political liberals are more likely to be religiously unaffiliated.

These findings do not surprise me. We have known for years that attendance in mainline churches are in decline. Even the more

1. Smith et al., "Religious Landscape Study."

What's Faith Got to Do With It?

contemporary churches have lost members, although at a slower pace than the traditional mainline denominational congregations. There is not a church that doesn't want to appeal to younger members. Yet, for many reasons younger people are not going to church. One of the reasons I have heard in conversations through the years is, "The church is so judgmental." When asked what that means, words like "control," "guilt," "obligation," "shame," "intellectually narrow," and "politically conservative" are often raised. This is driving people, particularly the young and more progressive, away.

And yet, whether people are going to church or not, they have their questions. They want to ask about life and death, life after death, prayer, and what faith even means. Some who have left the church have expressed that they miss it. They seek community. Even if they don't know what they believe, or if they don't like church doctrine or dogma, people want to make connections with others about shared values, hopes, and dreams. They may not like going to church, sitting in the pews, listening to hymns, choirs, and sermons, but they like going deep into the mysteries, and they love the questions!

Yes, there are some who have a very negative opinion of any religion. Yet, I have found that most are not anti-religion/faith/church, just anti-judgmentalism and anti–narrow intellectual thinking. If the church were less of a community of doctrine and dogma and more of a community of social engagement, nonjudgmental hospitality, support and accountability, spiritual nurture, and intellectual challenge open to questions and personal experience, then the church might become a moral center for faith and action for those who are seeking or drifting away. It may take the destruction of the institution to revitalize the church.

Alice, who I call my "bonus" daughter because she has been part of our family for many years, recently wrote me this email (used with permission) in response to an article I had published about prayer.[2]

---

2. Lentz, "What Good Is Prayer?"

Taking the Questions Seriously

This week I caught up on your newsletter and wanted to share how much I'm enjoying reading it. . . . I, of course, had some level of understanding of your relationship to religion and Christianity, but it's really cool to learn more about the nuances you think and feel about Jesus, God, prayer, the Bible, and the realities of Christianity in this world.

I was a product of an atheist household. . . . I felt strongly that God wasn't real, prayer was naive, and that religion was plainly to blame for so much of the world's present and historical conflict. . . . Over the past 3–5 years, as my consciousness around spirituality and the divine has expanded . . . I've been able to really appreciate and relate to why you (and really all religious/spiritual people!) connect with and/or follow a religion and commit yourself to a religious community.

Your article about prayer, from a month ago, really resonated with me. Prayer is maybe the area where I see my evolution of thinking on religion related most clearly. When I was younger, let's say 16 years old, if you told me I would one day sincerely use prayer as a practice, even if occasionally, I don't think I'd have believed you. Yet here I am! So far, I mostly only pray when I'm in a class or workshop and the yoga/meditation/spiritual teacher invites it. But I'm inspired by the way you explain prayer as a way to put energy into the universe, as a way to foster connection with yourself, those around you, a way to expand your imagination, and a way to spark action really spoke to me. I feel excited to experiment with more intentionally incorporating prayer into my life. . . . Anyway, thanks for reading! And for continuing to share your wisdom with the world in the name of spreading compassion and promoting humanity and justice for all.[3]

It meant so much to me to hear this bright young woman engage in such a manner. I doubt Alice will ever become an active member of a church or identify as a Christian. Yet, her response to me is an indication that the search for meaning goes through curiosity, honest reflection, questioning, doubt, coming back to

---

3. Alice, email message to author, Nov. 26, 2024.

things again and again, not being satisfied with easy answers, and just being truthful with where you are at every stage. Of note to me is that Alice was "excited to experiment," seeking new ways of practicing her beliefs and expressing her worldview.

Alice's words have encouraged me to continue my own journey of honest reflection, questioning, doubt and then coming back to things again and again, not being satisfied with easy answers, and just being truthful with where I am at this stage of my life. I too am excited to experiment with new ways of seeking and understanding!

Through the years I have had many conversations with people, like Alice, who are curious about going deeper into spiritual and religious matters.

Jill, a good friend, asked me many years ago, "What do I have to believe to be a Christian?" Jill was raised in the Jewish tradition. Yet, she was "religion fluid," having explored many religious traditions. I wasn't surprised by Jill's question, but I stumbled giving her a good answer.

Ask a more evangelical, fundamentalist Christian and one will get a traditional response. "What do I have to believe to be a Christian?" "You have to believe that Jesus is the Son of God. He was crucified and died for your sins. He was raised from the dead." If you believe in Jesus, which often is described as having a personal relationship with him, you will go to heaven when you die. One might refer to an ancient creed, for example the Nicene Creed or the Apostles' Creed, which add a belief in Jesus' birth from the Virgin Mary and that Jesus will return to judge both the living and the dead. Belief in the Bible as the inspired word of God is also fundamental to the traditional response.

That's a lot to get your mind and heart around. For most folks these descriptions of what Christian beliefs mean raise a lot of questions. Do you have to believe all of that or some of that? Are some things more important than others to believe in? Someone once asked me, "Am I a Christian if I believe that Jesus was a holy man and teacher who pointed to a way of experiencing the divine but don't really believe in all that heaven and hell stuff?" I would say, "Yes!" But many would contend that the person's profession doesn't go nearly far enough.

Almost all answers to Jill's question have something to do with "believing." Believe in Jesus, and you will be saved. Believe that you are a sinner and in need of God's grace. Believe in the virgin birth and the bodily resurrection of Jesus after his crucifixion. But what if you have questions about what any of this means? What does "believe" mean? Does "believe" mean accepting something as factually and scientifically true, even if you are not sure, or disagree, and it can't be proven? Or might it mean something broader? Belief for me is more a matter of the heart than it is of the head. I think something can be "true" without necessarily being "factual."

For example, the truth of a poem lies in its metaphorical description. I can believe in an idea that makes a huge difference in the way I live. I shape my worldview by that which I give my heart to what I "believe" and trust to be true. What I believe is my fundamental "North Star" guiding me in life.

There are those who have a cynical worldview. I have heard it crudely put, "Life sucks and then you die." If this is what you "believe," it will shape your living. If you "believe" that it is a "dog-eat-dog world," that too will shape how you respond to others and to life. If you believe that nothing that you do matters, that will affect how you live day to day. On the other hand, if you "believe" that there is a purpose to creation, that all humans are valuable, that it is good to be alive, and that being honest, peaceful, and generous are good things, that will make a difference too.

So, when Jill asked me, "John, what do I have to believe to be a Christian?" I didn't give a definitive answer. As I have reflected upon the question, I don't think there is an easy and definitive answer to give.

Answering Jill's question, on a superficial level, is fairly easy. Being a Christian is centered on Jesus. Being a Christian is seeking to follow his teachings. Being a Christian means circling the mystery and reality of resurrection (that Jesus rose from the dead). Some would say that there is a lot more one *has to* believe to be part of the historical Christian faith. However, let's leave it there for now.

But the words *have to* often imply something more. Not just descriptive but proscriptive. Traditionally, orthodox faith requires certainty of answers. Orthodoxy (correct, right, true, straight opinion) usually means the acceptance of historical doctrine defined by creeds and councils from centuries ago. Correct as opposed to incorrect. Right as opposed to wrong. True as opposed to false. Straight as opposed to crooked or meandering.

My experience has never been so binary. The relationships I have made through the years indicate to me that I am far from being alone in my experience. Curious people (of Christian faith or otherwise) recognize nuance; they seek variations on a theme; they want to circle around the mysteries and seek multiple interpretations. For me, being curious is more important than being certain. I am fascinated by other religions and want to learn from them. I don't "believe" that Christianity provides the only path to truth, although it does present a unique take on suffering, redemption, and how to describe God.

For example, I have had many experiences of bumping into a "truth" like "God is love," which pointed beyond itself to another series of questions leading to new "truths." How do you love someone you do not like and cannot stand? How do you love your enemy?

I describe my own faith as a journey of curiosity and discovery, raising new questions, leaving me hungering for more. My hunch is that this perspective is attractive to many, both believer and seeker.

I have encountered many Christians who attend conservative, evangelical churches who have their doubts and questions, but they don't feel confident to express their concerns. Or, if they do express themselves, they are quick to retreat when someone in authority gives a standard answer: "Well the Bible says . . ."

So, returning to Jill's question, I am not sure what you have to believe. There have always been a multitude of ways to attempt to answer questions of faith. However, individuals and groups who have strayed beyond the norm and come up with different answers to the questions and have sought to express their beliefs in different ways have often faced rejection or worse.

As one who loves and has studied history, I can understand the development of Christian thought through the ages: each curious theologian and biblical scholar building and expanding on what they understood the Bible to be teaching and on what prior scholars had written and taught. Unfortunately, in my opinion, those who held (and still hold) power sought to narrow the possible answers to the multitude of questions arising in the first centuries of the faith. The goal was to organize, define, limit, and control the new energy and enthusiasm of the first believers. Therefore, a set of rules and meanings was established.

Inevitably, the move to limit answers led to oppression and violence that we struggle with to this day. We try to "box" God into formulaic statements. We try to control the story of Jesus lest people get too radical! We stress the Jesus meek and mild at the expense of the Jesus who turned over the tables in the temple courtyard and preached of a "kingdom (or empire) of God," which was a political threat to the "empire of Rome."[4]

One of the issues that has always bedeviled the seeker is that the history of the early church is replete with horrific stories of what the growing church institution did to those who were not deemed orthodox. The so-called heretics, who pushed against the institutional orthodoxy, were, if lucky, kicked out of the church. If not so lucky, they were condemned to death.

In American history, the use of the Bible to defend the enslavement of Africans is damning testimony against the so-called Christian culture that claims to follow Jesus. For some, this history of racist violence, domination, and oppression is reason enough not to enter the doors of any church. Violence against the LGBTQA+ community and individuals in many places in the name of Christianity shows that the virulent strain of violent Christianity is still very much with us today. While not (yet) as violent in contemporary America, Christians still debate what is right belief and defend their orthodoxy and, in most cases, leave the violence to the

4. Crossan, *God and Empire*, 97–142.

next life. Yet, marginalized persons are scared to enter churches even now. The virulent language coming from some pulpits during elections supporting violence against the press, immigrants, and other marginalized communities follow the historical pattern of "otherizing" and misrepresenting the message of Jesus.

Self-proclaimed Christian nationalists believe that they should take power and influence every aspect of political, religious, and social life in the name of Jesus. To me and to most, this hubris shows their blatant disregard for the teachings and experience of Jesus who refused the temptation to rule, and who himself was crucified by the oppressive hand of the imperium.

There are Christians who support the modern state of Israel because they believe that Jesus will return only when Jews reclaim the historic boundaries of the kingdom of David and Solomon. However, the support is hardly benign. According to these Christians, Jews who do not convert to Christianity face hellfire and damnation when Jesus returns. Only Christianity will survive, dominate, and win.

With these expressions of Christian faith, is it any wonder why so many thoughtful people want nothing to do with Christianity? Alice is correct that the church has supported war and terror through the ages. Jill's question is complicated by historic reality. And yet, Alice and Jill and so many others still lean into the questions, intuitively understanding that the present dominant strain of Christianity is not the only one.

There is a disconnect between the church and its creeds. The words don't match the deeds. The old traditional answers to the myriad of questions being raised today as people are seeking and searching for a life of meaning, community, and purpose are not satisfying to me and to many others. All of this can leave the person who is Christian, Christian adjacent, interested, and leaning into knowing more about Jesus and his teachings confused and not pursuing faith: "If this is what I have to believe, I am not sure I want it."

Taking the Questions Seriously

As the late Professor Marcus Borg described in his book *The Heart of Christianity*,[5] the traditional paradigm of faith had, as its goal, heaven: the place where Christian believers go after death. Heaven is the reward for right belief. Hell, in opposition, described often as the place of fiery torment where there is "wailing and gnashing of teeth," is the place where folks who have the "wrong" belief and non-Christians go. Life is defined as a zero-sum game. Hence you must believe the right things. You must have the correct answers.

But life and faith are not binary experiences or simple black-and-white choices. We are all walking paths not completely known, often squinting to search for a way. The prayer of Thomas Merton is ever helpful to the faithful seeker. He admits that he "doesn't see the road" in front of him, and he doesn't know "where it will end." He can't be sure he is following the path of God. Yet, his journey of a prayerful life leads him to a wonderful insight: the desire to please God is pleasing to God. Therefore, he can move through life not in fear but fascination.[6] Merton's wisdom should be a guide for us all.

Merton's prayer uses several words that are synonyms of "faith." He uses the word "trust" and "belief," "desire" and "knowing." All these words are very helpful for our journey, helping to broaden our understanding. Merton suggests a way of describing faith that is shaped by an understanding of the Hebrew word for "belief," *emunah* (eh-moo-nah). The word can be translated as "faith" or "steadfastness" but implies movement. *Emunah* literally means "to take firm action," so having faith is more than presuming intellectual certainty or confidence in doctrinal statements, it is a verb—an action word. It implies that your faith is found in locomotion. The word that is used to end prayers, "Amen," shares the root with *emunah* and means "may it be so." Or perhaps, "Let's get moving and make it happen!"[7]

---

5. Borg, *Heart of Christianity*, 7–12.
6. Merton, *Thoughts on Solitude*, 79.
7. Brown et al., *Hebrew and English Lexicon*, 53.

What's Faith Got to Do With It?

The Greek word for belief is *pistis*, which is translated "faith," "firm persuasion," "assurance," "firm conviction," or "faithfulness."[8] In the New Testament, the Greek word *pisteuo* is used to describe believing in Jesus and having eternal life. *Pisteuo* means to completely rely on Jesus and be willing to do whatever he instructs, which includes entrusting one's life to him and surrendering one's heart to him.

I contend that something of the fullness of the meaning of "belief" and "faith" is lost when the emphasis of the Greek word is stressed over that of the nuances of the word in Hebrew. Thomas Merton's prayer reflects the Hebrew sense of moving forward, trusting but not necessarily knowing all the details.

The stories of the New Testament show that Jesus had *emunah*—a steadfastness, taking firm action even in the midst of real doubt. The scene of Jesus in the garden of Gethsemane (Mount of Olives, Mark 14:32–42) on the night of his arrest, recorded in the Gospels, suggests not a firm conviction as much as a hanging-on-in-the-midst-of-great-anguish faith.

Yet, for contemporary Christians, anguish, doubt, and having questions is often interpreted as a weakness instead of a strength. Instead of promoting the active faith *of* Jesus, Christianity has emphasized faith *in* Jesus. Not that those are unrelated or mutually exclusive, but emphasis matters. I believe that emphasizing Jesus, the man who trusted God, who gave his heart to a new vision of heaven and earth, and who struggled, doubted, wondered, took risks, welcomed the marginalized, and refused to be drawn in to the systems of privilege and power, is far more appealing to most of us today, whether or not we call ourselves Christian.

Alice and Jill are two people who were not raised in the Christian church and yet are open to a conversation shaped by their experiences and curiosity. They love the questions and seek after answers that make sense to them in the here and now. I think they show us the way forward.

---

8. Bauer et al., "πίστις," *Greek-English Lexicon*, 660–61.

CHAPTER 2

James, Madelaine, and the Group

MY CONVERSATIONS WITH ALICE and Jill were mirrored in the fascinating discussion I had with Madelaine and James, who, with their questions and their two young daughters, found themselves drawn to the Christian community. "When I was growing up my mother said that all religion was a cult, particularly Christianity, and that we should stay clear of church." So said Madelaine as I sat at her kitchen table with her and her husband, James. Madelaine, James, and their two young children started coming to Forest Hill Church, Presbyterian, in Cleveland Heights, Ohio, as soon as the Covid restrictions were lifted and in-person worship began again. Madelaine has a doctorate in medieval music, studied in Italy, and has sung professionally. James is an equally gifted violinist. The church's music director knew talent when she heard it. The director of family, youth, and children welcomed the girls into Sunday school.

Madelaine and James are intelligent and thoughtful people with more than a touch of skepticism for pat answers and easy solutions. James, Madelaine, and their daughters became part of the community but were hesitant to join the church and not ready to attend any new member classes. They felt a sense of belonging, appreciating the church's hospitality, but as far as believing anything specific, they weren't ready for that.

They reacted negatively to what research has shown to be a common concern expressed in the recent Pew Research study.[1] James and Madelaine didn't like the judgmental, patriarchal, narrow language of what many perceive to be standard Christianity. They had gay, lesbian, and transgender friends and didn't want to be part of any community that would exclude or demean people who were important to them. They had many questions about faith in general and Christianity in particular. They wanted their questions to be taken seriously and not swept aside by "Well, to be a Christian you have to believe . . ."

Questions of heaven and hell, salvation, and the multitude of beliefs that Christians traditionally hold interested them intellectually but didn't move them to join a church. They questioned what the title "Lord" meant—"so medieval." "'Savior.' What does that mean?" "Saved from what for what?" They had many questions about the history of doctrine and why there are so many creeds and so many denominations and why Protestants and Catholics split apart. I loved being with them.

At our first kitchen table conversation, James pulled out his cell phone and read to me the list of questions that he and Madelaine had compiled. There were questions about sin, heaven and hell, and why the church was so concerned about sex. There were questions about why different churches did what they did during the worship service (liturgy). Why did ministers wear robes? There were questions about Jesus—his life, his death. They asked what I thought was the most pressing question: "What is the added value of being a Christian?" That question got to the heart of my seeking too: "So what? Does being a Christian matter?"

Even with all their questions, Madelaine and James came to church each Sunday. The girls attended Sunday school. They appreciated the progressive sermons. They loved participating in the music program. Their girls were happy at the church and often encouraged their parents to take them on Sunday. They supported

1. Smith et al., "Religious Landscape Study."

the church's commitment to social action and the mission of the congregation.

Yet, it was still a surprise to me when they signed up for the new members class. At the first class the participants shared a little bit about their personal faith journey and what brought them to this moment. Madelaine and James told their stories, the other members of the class nodding their heads in appreciation of James's and Madelaine's experience. The first class covered the history of the congregation, its mission statement, and a bit about what it means to be a Presbyterian and an active church member. The next week we described the process of becoming an active member and described what would happen during the worship service when they joined the church.

There are three ways of becoming an active member of the Presbyterian church:

1. Transfer of membership (moving from one congregation to another)
2. Profession of faith (the person is baptized but has no church affiliation)
3. Baptism

Everyone in the class had been baptized, except for Madelaine.

After the class, Madelaine and I agreed that she should not rush into baptism. Skeptical of church dogma and doctrine to begin with, she didn't want to confess to things she wasn't sure of, use words that she didn't understand, and become a member of an institution that she had always rebelled against.

I gave her Marcus Borg's *The Heart of Christianity* to read. Madelaine and I planned to have two or three conversations to discuss her questions and concerns. There was no need to rush what is a very significant act. Being baptized carries with it a response to some questions about the identity and status of Jesus. It means making a public declaration that you want to be part of the church—yes, to an individual local congregation but also to the historical and worldwide church with all its glory and not so glorious baggage.

Over the next few weeks, we talked about her questions and reshaped the traditional language about "Lord" and "Savior." Madeleine was more comfortable with the language found in the Gospel of John, of following "the way, the truth, and the life" of Jesus (John 14:6). By that she meant that Jesus modeled a life of hospitality and compassion, exemplifying a spiritual discipline of prayer and action. She said that she could affirm this faith statement and would be baptized and become an active member of the church if the changes to the language was acceptable to the congregational leaders.

The Session of the Church (the governing body of lay leaders) approved Madelaine's reworking of the traditional questions and accepted her profession of faith. Madelaine's focus on the life of Jesus rather than on words about Jesus' status excited and challenged the members of the Session, many of whom shared that they too had been put off by language and titles about Jesus.

A few Sundays later, in handmade matching dresses, Madelaine was baptized along with her two daughters. Then Madelaine and her husband, James, joined seven other individuals and became active members of the church. It was one of the most meaningful baptisms of my career. I was reminded of the words that were used at the baptism of a little girl: "Little sister, by this act of baptism, we welcome you to a journey that will take your whole life. This isn't the end. Where God will take you, surprise you, we cannot say. This we do know and this we say: God is with you."

The results of the Pew study on the religious landscape, the response of Alice, the question that Jill raised, the table conversation with Madelaine and James, and her baptism indicated to me that there is an exciting way forward by raising the questions and leading with curiosity. I concluded that the shared experiences that people have, the questions people raise, the doubts that are expressed, and the anti-institutional reactions are actually not signs of a decline in faith but an indication of resurgence and hopefulness. People want new ways of addressing age-old questions. They don't want to be limited by pat answers often given by religious leaders who may not be sure of the answers themselves.

My thesis that people are not turned off by religion but rather are looking for on-ramps to faith and community was supported by the discussion group I led with fifteen young church members who were not hesitant to share their faith journeys and to raise their questions. The participants were mostly white, had been raised in the church, and were well-educated and upper middle class, although there was one person who grew up in the Buddhist tradition in Asia, a couple who had lived most of their lives in Ghana, and three who had only nominal association with a religious community growing up. All the participants were now members of Forest Hill Church, Presbyterian. They were all very positive about their experience at their current church community.

However, both those who had grown up within a faith community and those who were raised without a religious upbringing shared mostly negative views about what they experienced, saw, and were taught. With one exception, everyone expressed their memory of their religious upbringing as being shaped by the emphasis upon sin and going to hell. The message they received was, "You'd better behave or else." Martha shared that she remembers being told, "God is always watching you. When you are in your room and try to do something, even though your parents are not looking at you, God is looking at you." What was clear in her words and expressions was that God watching you was not seen as a positive.

Katherine remembered that her church split up after a bad relationship between the two pastors. The priority of the church seemed to be "self-preservation and financial security." There was not a high level of trust among the members.

Sheryl, who had been raised as a Buddhist, remembers her experience of that faith as superficial: "We had to identify [as Buddhist] on a self-identification government document." Those who explored other faiths, particularly Christianity, were frowned upon. Christians were not allowed to practice Buddhist rituals. She shared that she was forbidden to go to church even just to see what it was about. When she came to America, she began to play the organ at a local congregation. She was drawn to the community. However, church members were judged negatively for dating non-Christians.

Madelaine didn't tell her parents that she was getting baptized. "They would be mad." However, she believed that her father sought some kind of spirituality. Her mother once said to her, "Oh yes, he sometimes asks me, 'Shouldn't we figure this out before we die? Shouldn't we talk about what's next?'" But Madelaine shared that her mother told her father to shut up.

What was important to Madelaine's faith journey was her time of study in Italy. She said, "If you took the religion out of this country, there would be nothing left. You wouldn't have churches, you wouldn't have music, you wouldn't have the paintings." She was drawn by the history and the culture. Singing the ancient masses moved her. It wasn't the doctrine or the dogma, rather it was the art and music. She expressed, "I wanted something. I wanted a power beyond me, and I didn't want to be alone."

James, whose father was a nominal Presbyterian and whose mother was a nominal Roman Catholic, remembers nothing other than some "vague notion that God is love." When he went to college, he was perplexed by the "strong, amazing, powerful young women" who were conservative Christians who believed that they were "second to men." He was really turned off. He decided that faith was about moral behavior and asked, "Why do I need to believe in God or Jesus to be a moral person?"

"I was baptized as a child but I don't remember going to church at all," Dee Dee said. As a teen she attended a youth group which was a good experience for her. "The message I remember receiving was a lot about community. The youth group? It was like the misfit toys. Anybody could come. It didn't matter. We prayed, we sang, but it didn't matter if you didn't believe. It didn't." She recalled going on a trip with the youth group to another church but was turned off by that church's emphasis on hell. "I didn't like that at all."

Jake was raised Roman Catholic and went to church twice a week. "I literally remember hearing, 'If you don't believe this, you will go to hell. If you do not take Communion, you will go to hell.' Hell was big. There was a constant focus on what you had done that was wrong." Jake "broke away" from this rigid background when he went to a secular college. "It was just so unrealistic for the world that I was confronted with. Compared to the realities I was seeing in college. I was exposed to more diversity and more freedom of thought."

Beatrice, raised in Ghana, remembered what she called the "Old Testament Church," which emphasized what you wore and not bringing "bad spirits into the church." The church of her youth emphasized the elevated status of men: "They sat in a different place, and men read the Scriptures and led the prayers."

Kurt grew up in the Presbyterian church, "but sin was still front and center." When he went to college, he joined a Christian fellowship. He shared a memory of all-night theological discussions: "We would stay up all night arguing about how you get into heaven. You had to have the correct theology. Back then it was all about whether you believed in a pre-trib or post-trib apocalypse."[2]

Amy, the oldest member of the group, shared a similar experience. When asked about her church experience she said, "Ugh!" "Like a lot of you, I grew up in the church because that's where my family went. I married a guy whose father and grandfather and all his uncles were Methodist ministers. Church for me was just, you know . . . something you did because of family history and all." However, it was Amy's description of her coming to understand faith and church in a new way that reshaped the conversation.

The turning point for Amy and her husband came one Sunday as they looked around and "saw all these old people who were of a very different political persuasion than we were. We stopped

---

2. *Pre-* and *post-tribulation* are ways that some Christians answer the question about the end time (eschatology) and when Jesus is coming back. The tribulation is a period of great suffering and persecution. Some verses in Revelation, Daniel, and Mark suggest that Jesus will come back before this tribulation and rescue believers, while other verses suggest that Jesus will return after this time of hardship.

going." However, after their children were born, Amy and her husband decided to go back to church. The church they found changed everything. "It was the first time that I felt church was a real community. I had a sense of a diverse, inclusive, loving, thought-provoking place. From then on, that is what's important to me—its community and building relationships. There is the faith piece and the God piece, but it's about being in community with other people. Yes, Jesus loves you. God loves you. But you're also part of a great community of people who believe in something bigger than themselves, seeking to live like Jesus and to do good in the world." Amy's words resonated with those gathered. She continued, "If you are isolating and not with other people, then you probably aren't going to be a good person. You can argue yourself into any position, some people do, but having other people support you and hold you accountable is really important. You need to stay a functional human, and you need others to tell you if you're not being nice and work on a way to get back on track. So yeah, isolation is bad."

Em was the one person who had a uniformly positive experience of faith and church growing up. She was raised in rural Indiana in the Church of the Brethren Anabaptist denomination.[3] Her experience was shaped by a strong sense of community and social justice. She recalled going to peace protests and becoming engaged in environmental justice. She would sing and raise money to save the rainforest. It wasn't about doctrine and dogma but service. It wasn't about control, hell and damnation, or right theology. Faith to Em was about joy and community and service. To Em, this is what the Bible taught and how Jesus lived. She attended Quaker services and then worshiped at a large nondenominational praise church. She attended an all-Black church and developed a love of gospel music.

---

3. Anabaptists are a Christian movement originating in the sixteenth century that emphasized adult baptism. They rejected the authority of state churches and advocated for a separation of church and state. Key Anabaptist beliefs include pacifism and a commitment to living according to the teachings of Jesus.

James, Madelaine, and the Group

When I asked the group—particularly wanting those who had a negative experience of faith and church to respond—why they still attended, the answer was uniform. They all sought community, a shared identity, a family. They didn't want judgment, guilt, or shame. They sought, joy, creativity, and engagement in the world. They didn't want doctrine or dogma, although they yearned to understand what it all meant. They didn't feel the need to be told that they were sinners who needed to be saved. They were unanimous that they wanted to know that they were beloved children of God, and so was everybody else. They weren't suspicious of other religions and faith perspectives. They, in the words of Amy, wanted to be held accountable to being good people.

Kurt, who had shared his memories of all-night theological discussions about the end time, said, "As time passed, I found another church. Week after week a gentle preaching about loving one another. Over years and years and years of that, I concluded that I had been thinking too much about the wrong things. I remember thinking one day and asked myself, 'If you could prove to me that God didn't exist, that none of what we do is real, what would you do tomorrow morning?' My answer? The same thing I'm doing today. I'd be right here singing in the choir on Sunday. It's about how we treat people, how we look at people. You may not look like me, but you are a beloved child of God every bit as much as I am and every bit as much as everybody else. But what do we need to believe? I don't know. I mean, this is the community of misfits that I'm hanging out with."

What everyone agreed to was this: being a Christian meant loving one another and treating others as you would want to be treated. They all wanted to believe in goodness but not in a binary heaven and hell. Goodness transcended all religions. Katherine expressed what many affirmed, "My hippie non-god-believing mom always says, 'Love is an action word.' Jesus is an example. I don't know if you even have to believe in Jesus—like did he exist?—I still think that's one of the questions that all of us wonder about, but I believe in what Jesus stood for. You don't have to be perfect.

What's Faith Got to Do With It?

That's an image of Christianity that I'm still developing or at least wrapping my head around."

Madelaine summed it up: "What I see is that most churches have their own doctrines. They push people away who don't believe like they do. But how is anyone going to believe if they are not allowed to come in where they see the love and hear the words?"

I hope that you, the reader, have picked up on some of the common threads. Certainly, there was in the stories shared an emphasis that the Christian faith was about a certain kind of behavior. While there were experiences of being welcomed and accepted, underlying most of the comments was a strain of judgment and promised punishment if you didn't behave. God was watching. God was like your mother and father. You couldn't smoke or have sex. Leadership roles and participation were divided by gender. Even in Katherine's church, which was well ahead of its time in calling a woman co-pastor, division split the church. Church members and leaders behaved badly. Congregational life was often more about self-protection than following the call to justice and inclusion. Eugene Peterson in his book *Under the Unpredictable Plant* writes, "Most religion is not gospel. Most religion is idolatry. Most religion is self-aggrandizement."[4] I believe Peterson is correct. The comments of many in the group seemed to support this description. Perhaps Amy said it best when she and her husband came to the conclusion that church was . . . well, "Ugh!"

And yet, despite the criticisms of the church, the sense of being judged, the narrow traditionalism of many congregations, the cliquishness that formed among churchgoers, and not finding places where their deep personal questions could be safely raised, these younger adults sought to be part of something larger, a community. They wanted safe space to know more and get clearer about what they believed to be true, without hearing, "You're wrong." They all wanted to make a connection between their personal and public life. They wanted a balance between the spiritual and the intellectual. They wanted to be held accountable to standards

---

4. Peterson, *Under the Unpredictable Plant*, 46.

of generous living that they didn't easily find in their day-to-day work, play, and relationships.

Above all, they were curious. My sense was, after this meeting, that no one would be satisfied by a narrow, proscriptive answer to the question, "What do you have to believe to be a Christian?" However, there was clearly a desire to go deeper and understand the history and framework of why Christians use the language they use and do what they do. They wanted to know more about Jesus, the Bible, the church, sin, and their place in the world. They had questions about prayer and worship. Clearly, issues of faith matter to them. They wanted new words to express traditional ideas.

The group that gathered around the table was small. Everyone was associated with Forest Hill Church, a faith community that is recognized as a "liberal and progressive" congregation. The group was homogeneous. It makes me wonder if the format and questions would work in other congregational contexts where members have self-selected around issues of common identity and thought. And for the audience of seekers and skeptics? I don't know. This conversation format would probably not hold up to social scientific methods of study. But my guess is that the experiences of the people around the table in the fellowship hall would resonate with those who have different experiences of the church or who have left the church or never entered a sanctuary.

The experience of leading this exercise affirmed my seeking for language to describe my own faith. It confirmed my desire to look again at the questions, to love and live the questions, to lead with curiosity until I bumped into something that pointed the way.

Chapter 3

Loving the Questions

The important thing is not to stop questioning. Curiosity has its own reason for existing. One cannot help but be in awe when one contemplates the mysteries of eternity, of life, of the marvelous structures of reality. It is enough if one merely tries to comprehend a little of this mystery every day. Never lose a holy curiosity.

—Albert Einstein, *Life* magazine, May 2, 1955

Becoming is better to being.

—Paul Klee, *The Diaries of Paul Klee 1898–1918*

The journey is my home.

—Nikos Kazantzakis, *Report to Greco*

I WAS PROFOUNDLY MOVED by the experiences shared by the group during the first session. What I noticed was a common longing to be part of a community that wanted to move beyond narrow doctrine, dogma, and cultural expectation. Amy said it best about being part of a community where you are recognized, accepted, loved, and held accountable. This community is welcoming, socially active and doesn't take itself too seriously. This community recognizes shared fundamental values, encourages living the faith you have and being honest about the faith you aren't quite sure of.

The questions raised during the group conversation were too numerous to list them all. However, the questions could be grouped around several key areas.

There were many questions about the Bible. Most of the group members confessed that they didn't read the Bible often. They read along during the Scripture readings before the sermon. One person said that they had attempted to read the Bible from cover to cover but stopped somewhere in Judges.

Some wondered how the Bible came to be. "Why did some books make it and others didn't?" Others wanted to know if the cultural patriarchy of the ancient world created barriers to a modern engagement with the sacred texts. "How can the Bible be pertinent to us if it reflects the Mediterranean culture of two thousand to four thousand years ago?" One asked, "What makes the Bible sacred?" This question led to rapid-fire follow-up queries: "Do we read the Bible literally or not?" and "Were the writers of the Bible divinely inspired or were they writing from their own experience?" Another asked, "Why are there so many different Bible translations and paraphrases, and what is the difference? Are some better than others?"

There were many questions asked about God. No one in the group questioned God's existence, but they did wonder about how God is present and active in the world today. The question of human suffering, particularly the question of why "good people" suffer, came up often. One question, that I believe was shaped by the Christian belief that Jesus suffered and died for the sins of the world, was, "Does God suffer?" "Is God larger than Christianity?" one asked.

Trying to figure out what God wants and how to communicate with God were on the minds of several people. "Who has a line to God?" "Who can/can't talk to God?" "Do we need God and

Jesus to be moral?" A related question was, "Did the moral code we live by even come from God?"

The group wanted to know about Jesus—"Who was he?" "How is Jesus a savior?" "Was he a prophet, teacher, oppressed person?" Several were very concerned by the politicizing of Jesus in the context of the 2024 presidential election. "Has there been a political hijacking of Jesus?" This person expressed a deep worry about Jesus being used by white Christian nationalists. One, who had grown up in a more conservative evangelical church, wanted to know more about what happened on the cross. "What does it mean that Jesus died for our sins? I just don't get it."

Many shared their confusion and frustration about the church, its language and practices. There was a strong shared critique of the hierarchy of the institution and its emphasis on judgment, guilt, and shame. One wondered if the church and its weekly worship service got in the way of a deeper spirituality.

Questions about prayer were raised by many. "Can we ask God for things?" "What is prayer?" "Why do we recite the Lord's Prayer every Sunday?" "How does intercessory prayer work? Does it work?"

There was a lot of interest in talking about Christianity's relationship to other religions. Almost everyone at the table had friends who were Jewish, Muslim, Hindu, and Buddhist. While no one was comfortable, and some thought it absurd, that non-Christians went to hell—"What about all the good people: Jews, atheists, and folks who don't know?"—there was shared concern about the history of Christian violence against Jews. The questions asked pointed to a curiosity about Judaism, its practices and beliefs. There was real interest in understanding how Christianity had fulfilled, adopted, appropriated, and usurped the Jewish story and its rituals.

Many expressed a deep appreciation for the beliefs and practices of other faiths. No one disagreed that Christianity could learn a lot from other faith traditions. The question was raised, "Can we have confidence in Christianity when there are so many choices and differing interpretations?" "Is one more correct than the other?" "Can I be a Christian and participate in the prayers and practices of other faiths?" These questions indicated a real curiosity about how Christians live in a pluralistic society.

Some blamed Christianity for being the most divisive religion in today's world. It is hard to argue against this, particularly in the American context.

Sex and both the "purity culture" and the "bro culture" were topics of interest. The concern seemed to focus around two issues:

1. Gender and sexual identity and the socially conservative backlash
2. Sex being bad or sinful

Many expressed frustration that Christianity seemed to be a religion of rules and judgment, condemnation and shame. The issue of sexual misconduct of members of the clergy was raised and added to the opinion that the church was hypocritical about sex, sexual identity, and sexual practice.

There were theological questions about the nature of humanity, God, salvation, and how humans are supposed to live in the world? "What is the kingdom of God? Where is it?" "Can we be involved in 'worldly' things?" There was shared skepticism about the status of humans: "Are humans superior to other creatures?" "If God's spirit is present everywhere, is it in water?"

"What is the role of doubt?" "What happens after death? Before birth?" "Is there heaven and hell?" "What is grace?" "Do we have free will?" "Do we get credit for our intention versus action?" And finally, "What does faith/belief add? What is the point?" Yes indeed, what is the point?

If the group would have spent another hour together, I am sure there would have been many more questions. Very few of these questions have simple answers if any answer at all. Furthermore, these questions have inspired countless authors through the centuries to write countless books. Is another book even needed? Yet the people in the group, some of whom had read some of the books, found them too dogmatic, too academic, too confusing, almost as if the author was talking down to them.

What's Faith Got to Do With It?

I took some joy in this fact: young adults who had come to church that morning singing hymns, listening to the sermon, and taking communion felt liberated enough to stay and share what was on their minds, to admit their doubts and confusion to each other. If nothing else came of this, what a marvelous experience of what a church could be.

I was reminded of lyrics of the first verse of the hymn "Blest Be the Tie That Binds": "Blest be the tie that binds / our hearts in Christian love; / the fellowship of kindred minds / is like to that above."[1] We had formed a fellowship of kindred minds leaning into our shared questions, curious to listen to each other, safe in this nonjudgmental community. We didn't all agree. Some still wondered about their own faith. The questions of faith and doubt were all around us written on the newsprint hanging on the wall of the fellowship hall, inviting us to live and love them as we dug deeper.

I no longer think that coming up with definite answers is the goal. Rather, it is to lean in with curiosity to the questions. It is important to circle the mysteries and celebrate the journey of continual discovery and lifelong learning as the object of our desire to know. With each turn around, a new insight arises. Our temporal experience is challenged and encouraged by the eternal quest. In the sometimes dim mirror of our present realities, we catch a glimpse of some guidepost that leads us on. This is not to argue that there is no ultimate truth, only to suggest that the truth we perceive is partial, interpretive—pointing beyond. Emily Dickinson, an American poet of the mid-nineteenth century, advises that one should "tell all the truth but tell it slant," as in her poem by the same name.[2]

The goal of this book is to point to the larger truths as best I can, shaped by my experience, my hopes and doubts, with the slant of surprise and with kind and partial explanations that hopefully guide, encourage, and invite the reader to explore until they are dazzled by their own possibilities! Creators of their own collective realities that point onward.

1. Fawcett, "Blest Be the Tie That Binds," stanza 1.
2. Dickinson, "Tell All the Truth but Tell It Slant," *Complete Poems*, 506.

CHAPTER 4

Mapping the Journey

I can only tell you, for what it is worth, how I, personally, look at the matter....
...Do not mistake it for the thing itself: and if it does not help you, drop it.

—C. S. LEWIS, *MERE CHRISTIANITY*

Carry out your own salvation with fear and trembling.

—SAINT PAUL, PHILIPPIANS 2:12

I REMEMBER FIRST READING C. S. Lewis's *Mere Christianity* as a teenager. I found his practical, no-nonsense, "this is what I believe" style fresh and very helpful. Lewis wrote with such clarity and conviction, forceful yet inviting. He was, after all, an "apologist." Not the "I am sorry" definition of apology but the original Greek translation of the word which means to make a defense. He was defending the language and tradition of Christianity.

I returned to this book and many of C. S. Lewis's works again and again throughout my career. Yet, as my life and ministry developed, I found that Lewis's apology no longer fulfilled my questions and yearnings. While there is much to defend about the faith that has developed through the centuries, and *Mere Christianity* is still on my list of must-reads, Lewis was writing during and in the aftermath of World War II, when the world was in a binary struggle against the evils of the National Socialism of Hitler and those who called him the "savior of the world." This reality of world history shaped his faith and his writing.

I believe we need to continue to welcome new voices and perspectives that both defend and challenge orthodoxy and open ways of wondering that reveal deeper mysteries of faith.[1] As much as I was influenced, in my early years, by Lewis, I remember very clearly noticing the quotations that I placed at the beginning of this chapter. I don't think Lewis would go as far as I am going, but the words "if it does not help you, drop it" invite the seeker to other ways of looking at things, to test initial answers, and to question revealed truth in the light of life and experience. To be drawn again and again to the questions, to live the questions, to honor the seeking, to celebrate the, what I call, little findings of truth as you come to them. I commend Lewis for his humility when he writes, "I can only tell you, for what it is worth, how I, personally, look at the matter."[2] I believe that Lewis had the spirit of Paul of Tarsus, one of the first interpreters of Christian faith.

I compare Paul of Tarsus to one of my cinematic heroes, Indiana Jones. In the first installment of the movie series, *Raiders of the Lost Ark*, Jones is hunched behind a rock protecting himself from the Nazi troops transporting the ark of the covenant to Germany. Jones suddenly leaps on a horse, chasing the truck holding the ark. Jones's friend says, "Indie, what are you doing?" and Jones replies, "I am making it up as I go along."[3] I have always felt that this is the best way to describe the organizing chops of Paul.

---

1. See Manning, *Ragamuffin Gospel*; Bell, *Love Wins*; Held, *Searching for Sundays*.
2. Lewis, *Mere Christianity*, 61.
3. Spielberg, *Raiders*; my paraphrase.

Having had the transformative experience of the spirit of Jesus on the road to Damascus (Acts 9), Paul gives the rest of his life to traveling around the Roman Mediterranean world interpreting the questions of the first Christians. His answers were the best he could do at the time in the midst of diverse realities. Many of his answers are brilliant and continue to challenge the modern reader. Paul challenges the cultural binary divisions (men/women, Jew/Greek, slave/free) of his day (Gal 3:28). In so doing, he invites us to challenge the socially constructed binary divisions of our day. His inkling that salvation is not only for individuals but for the entire created order (Greek *panta*, "everything") stretches the common notion that only Christians go to heaven. In fact, many scholars believe that Paul didn't necessarily define himself as a Christian. Rather, he continued to see himself as a Jew, although reinterpreting Judaism through his experience with Jesus.

Paul was a man of his time (as we are people of our time), and so he expresses the larger cultural norms about slavery and the role of women.[4] But admitting this doesn't mean that Paul is to be ignored. Rather it is an argument precisely for why we need to continue questioning and yearning, never presuming we have final answers. Paul points us in a new direction. His writings urge us onward in the journey. The words of Bilbo Baggins in J. R. R. Tolkien's *Lord of the Rings* come to mind: "The Road goes ever on and on, down from the door where it began. Now far ahead the Road has gone. And I must follow, if I can."[5]

Reading the letters of Paul, it is not hard to see him developing his thoughts while he writes. His more narrow understanding of the role of women, for example, is stretched by his more cosmic sense of identity. The tragedy, in my opinion, is that orthodox Christianity has used Paul, indeed the whole New Testament, to narrow questions and limit discussion. Many Christians look to Paul for the final biblical answer rather than seeing his words as

---

4. In 1 Tim 6:1–3, Paul writes that slaves should respect their masters. In 1 Tim 2:8–15 and 1 Cor 14:34, Paul writes that wives should be in submission to their husbands and not speak in church.

5. Tolkien, *Fellowship of the Ring*, 44.

opening ways of answering the questions of the moment. I like Paul's words in Philippians: "Carry out your own salvation in fear and trembling" (Phil 2:12). I think that Paul meant "fear and trembling" not in terms of being scared that you might fail life's final exam, although many have interpreted these words in just that way. Rather, I interpret "fear and trembling" as "awe and wonder." Paul is telling the Philippian Christians to take what he has told them and shown them and keep working at it, dare I say, interpret and improve; come up with answers that better fit the situation. Instead of shutting off conversation and shutting down interpretations, Paul is inviting the first Christians (and us too) to continue the work of loving and living the questions and to share the work with a community.

I think it is important for me to set the following chapters within the framework of these opening paragraphs. For while I will seek to answer the questions asked, I do so only as an invitation for you to dig deep within yourself and find better answers. I share the spirit of Saint Paul and C. S. Lewis: if you don't like my answers, well then find your own. Get into small groups and share your thoughts. Questions of faith are not like math problems. They are more like writing prompts.

Before we begin, it is important to be very clear about what I am setting out to do. This is not a scholarly work, although my thoughts have been shaped by the works of many scholars through the years. It is a journey of discovery. It is more of a conversation in book form. Don't just take my word for it. I am sharing from my experience and how I think about these questions of faith. My hope is that you will be engaged in the process bringing your answers, questions, criticisms, and concerns along for the ride.

The sources for my attempted answers include the Bible, which I have been preaching and teaching from for forty years, hundreds of commentaries and books, primary sources from the first century, and the insights of countless numbers of individuals—clergy, scholar, and layperson. Furthermore, my attempts of making sense of the questions have also been formed by literary fiction and nonfiction, by movies and television shows, by music, art, travel, and hundreds of conversations through the years.

As you read ahead, think about who and what has influenced your life and your view of things: a person, a piece of art that has moved you, a song that has shaped your imagination, a book (particularly fiction or poetry) that has opened up for you a new way of seeing the world. Taking inventory of these sources is an important first step. These non-biblical, secular works often provide important commentary on the matters of head and heart. They add depth to your reading of the Bible as reading the Bible adds depth to your experience. Figuring out what you believe is a journey that deserves the fullness of human expression.

As mentioned above, all the following chapters are shaped by the actual questions that individuals asked in the small group. I begin with a brief chapter on God and questions on life after death. Then I move on to who Jesus was, how to read the Bible, Christianity among other religions, faith and politics, prayer, and sex. There is a chapter about the creeds and confessions of the church, and then I sum it all up and answer the question, "What do I have to believe?"

Chapter 5

God?

Inscrutable His ways are and immune
To catechism by a mind too strewn
With petty cares to slightly understand
What awful brain compels His
Awful hand.

—Countee Cullen, "Yet do I Marvel"

We had thought of God as the dispenser of all good things we would possibly desire. God has nothing to give at all except himself.

—Simon Tugwell, "Prayer"

Let's start with God.[1] A vast majority of individuals say that they believe in some kind of god, higher power, higher aspiration, or creative spiritual force. Some describe their conception of god

---

1. When writing about the divine figure of Judaism, Christianity, and Islam in this chapter, I use the word God with a capital G. When writing about a spirit, idea, or aspiration, I will use the word god with a lowercase g.

in more personal, anthropomorphic ways, while others emphasize an idea, or spirit.

Joan Osborne wrote a song entitled "One of Us" in 1995. The expanded title of the original was "What if God Was One of Us?"[2] The opening lyrics ask that eternal question and both reflect and challenge the anthropomorphic claim of Christianity. Osborne then wonders if God is a "slob" or a "stranger on a bus." She asks if this God calls the Pope in Rome.

In the opening verse, a multitude of extraordinary queries arise about the existence of a divine other. Osborne wonders if god is a person (is god like a slob on a bus). She asks, if there is a god does he (Osborne's gender word choice) talk to the Pope? She raises questions about the institutional church and hierarchical power. Her lyrics invite us into the journey of loving and living the question. Next time on a bus, take a look at the "slob" sitting next to you (or for that matter take a look in the mirror), and ponder her question about the divine presence in others and yourself.

The questions of who is God, what is God, where is God, etc. have been asked and sung about for millennia. The author of Genesis has a take different from the author of the book of Job. The God of Genesis is a creator, enjoying the creation and seeking a relationship with humans. The God of Job is distant, unknowable, testing Job, who considers himself faithful. The New Testament reinterprets the various ways that the Hebrew Scriptures describe God. Christians have traditionally described Jesus as God, or at least as the Son of God.

The members of the after-church discussion group raised these questions: "Do I have to believe in a God who is watching my every move, ready to punish me?" "How can God allow for the starvation of children in Gaza and in Sudan?" While expressing their discomfort at more traditional notions that God is some male judge on a throne, distant and remote, all participants expressed their desire for there to be a god—some spiritual force that animated life, some power that was beyond them, some sense of consistent reality that made sense of everything.

2. Osborne, "One of Us."

What's Faith Got to Do With It?

Sometime in the 1990s, I was cornered in the hallway of the First Presbyterian Church in Winchester, Virginia, by a flock of middle school students. Ambushed, with my back to the wall, they confronted me with this question: "Who made God?" I gave what was the typical response that a newly ordained associate pastor might give: "No one made God. God has always been, from the beginning. God created everything." They all tilted their heads to the side and gave me one of those looks that told me that the answer that I had given wasn't the one they wanted. So, they tried again: "Really, who made God?" Nervously I responded, "God made God." Both the kids and I knew that didn't fly. Just then, Bryan, a fun-loving and hilarious adult with a quick wit and infectious personality who volunteered with the youth groups, seeing that I was in a tight spot, came over for assistance. The kids turned on him: "Who made God?" Without hesitation Bryan said, "Dupont. They made everything else?" The kids were apparently satisfied and went away. I was saved for other questions on other days.

Questions about God immediately arise when a conversation begins around religion, church, and faith. Even the most devout Christians I have known, me included, stumble over how to describe with any satisfaction who God is, how God acts, and what God wants from us. Among the Abrahamic faiths (Judaism, Christianity, and Islam) God has been described as a mother hen, a heartbroken lover, compassionate, a creator, a judge, a king, and a savior. God is most commonly stereotyped as an older, physically "ripped" white guy with flowing beard and hair. God is in control of everything and yet seemingly can't control anything—the creation or its people. God is totally other, unchanging, beyond everything, and yet God is described as intimate, angry, close, involved, judgy, caring. I've known people who pray to God to find a parking spot on a crowded street, believing that God is intimately involved with every aspect of their lives. I have known people who want nothing to do with God.

At times, God comes across as fickle, flipping decisions and appearing emotionally unstable, as God's relationship with Israel shows—punishing one moment and forgiving the next. God is beyond sex and gender, and yet God has been called both "Father" and "Mother." In the Hebrew Scriptures God has no name, and yet there are many names offered to describe the divine.

In monotheistic religions there is only one God. And yet, the Hebrew name of God, "Elohim," suggests with its plural ending multiple gods. All of this is to say that there is a lot of room to maneuver when it comes to talking about and describing God.

The American poet Countee Cullen pondered the "awful" inscrutability (unknowability) of God as he reflected on the African American experience of the divine. How could there be a God who would allow slavery? Since World War II, any conversation about God must acknowledge the reality of the Holocaust and the question of how God could let it happen to his so-called "chosen people." The question of why God, who is traditionally described by terms such as all-powerful (omnipotent) and all-present (omnipresent), would allow so many bad, destructive things to happen to so many innocent, good people has driven many towards atheism.[3] Furthermore, the confident use of God's name to support war, violence, nationalism, and suppression of minorities adds to people's experience of not wanting anything to do with God or religion.

This is not a new phenomenon. Authors of books found in the Hebrew Scriptures and the New Testament wonder who and where God is.[4] At Jesus' crucifixion he is reported to have recited the opening lines from Ps 22; "My God, My God why have you forsaken me?" Jesus, the so-named "Son of God" is aware of God's absence.

Almost everyone has questions about God. There have been countless attempts to describe the indescribable.[5] However, as the Pew study indicates, even people who have drifted away from church and organized religion still hold on to the concept of some higher, spiritual power that is beyond human description. This is as good a description of God as it gets. God has been described

---

3. For instance, Bertrand Russell gave a public lecture at Battersea Town Hall on March 6, 1927, titled "Why I Am Not A Christian"; see also Dawkins, *God Delusion*.

4. In the Hebrew Scriptures, read Job and Pss 10, 42, 77, 88, and 104.

5. See Armstrong, *History of God*.

as the "ground of being" by Paul Tillich, one's "higher power" in the twelve steps of Alcoholics Anonymous, and one's highest aspirations. The American novelist Octavia Butler writes, "The only lasting truth is change. . . . God is Change."[6]

The ancient story in the Hebrew Bible of Moses' encounter with YHWH is more in line with the contemporary seekers than with orthodox theologians. Moses, in Exod 3, has an experience of a presence in the wilderness as his attention is caught by a bush that seems to be in flames but is not being consumed. In this story, Moses asks God, "What shall I call you?" God responds, "I Am Who I Am" (Exod 3:14). Or a different translation could be, "I Will Be Who I Will Be." The liberating and creative power of this story is that God cannot be contained or boxed in by any descriptive characteristic. This should allow you who "love the questions" to hold all answers loosely.

Jonathan Rauch, in his recent book *Cross Purposes: Christianity's Broken Bargain with Democracy*, writes of his rejection of Jewish faith and his notion of God. His words, I imagine, reflect the thoughts of many:

> I just knew that the idea of a big father in the sky who creates the entire universe yet attends minutely to man's everyday affairs makes no sense, and that the tales of the Bible could not possibly be true to life. . . . If the tales were true, they showed God and his followers doing some rotten and senseless things. Perhaps instead of rejecting the notion of a God, it is high time we rejected the narrow and limiting description of God that doesn't make sense.[7]

I agree with Rauch. Those whose heart and mind lead them to seek larger answers need to do away with "the narrow and limiting description of God." Speaking personally, I do not believe in a God who directs every action, controls every event, rewards and punishes according to prescribed and changing cultural norms.

Perhaps the best way to begin is to ask yourself how your life and actions reflect both your deepest convictions and highest

---

6. Butler, *Parable of the Sower*, 226.
7. Rauch, *Cross Purposes*, 2.

aspirations about God. Reflect upon your own experiences. I remember the Reverend Dr. William Sloane Coffin's response to a person who was trying to console him after the tragic death of his son. The person shared her own deepest angst: "How could God do this?" And Reverend Coffin responded that God didn't do it. Rather, he said, "God's heart was the first of all our hearts to break."[8] God would have been the first presence with Alex when he died. So, God as loving presence, not hovering puppeteer.

A mother whose son died by overdose wondered about the presence of God but declared that she saw God in the response of people: present, caring, loving, supportive. She took great comfort in her conviction that her son was now at peace with the source of all peace. The mother's response transformed the lives of others.

We all wonder how there can be a God that allows famine and the death of innocent children and parents. Sometimes I wonder if God is not waiting on us to stop the war and the inequitable way that food and medicine is distributed. Is suffering in the world evidence of no God or evidence of a lack of a human response to alleviate the suffering?

I've always found compelling the notion that is expressed in Christianity that if you want to know who God is, what God desires, and how we should act, then look at Jesus. We will have more to say about Jesus in the next chapter, but if there is anything to the Christian claim that Jesus shows who God is, then we see a God who shows priority for the poor, is present in suffering, welcomes the marginalized, and loves everyone. God doesn't direct the action as much as God is revealed in the action of the presence of love. The ultimately unknowable God is glimpsed in our engagement with one another. How you relate to others, how you spend your money, what your priorities are will indicate the kind of higher power you believe in. Do you seek to be hospitable, present to others, compassionate, loving, and forgiving? I think this indicates a sense of your god and higher motivation.

Like all questions of faith, one must begin with curiosity and imagination. One size does not fit all. Start with what you give your

8. Marks, "Alex's Death."

mind and heart to, what shapes your actions. This might sound heretical to some, but if you could imagine a god, what would that god be for you? What characteristics do you want your god to have? My understanding is that you would be joining the ancestors in circling the mystery and leaning into the questions of ultimate concern.

I have always understood the creation story in Gen 1 not to be a scientific description of creation (more on this in chapter 7, on how to read the Bible). Rather, I agree with the scholars who argue that the creation story in Genesis is a reworking of an earlier creation myth that described the creation of the earth as the result of the warfare in heaven among the gods. The Ugaritic creation story highlights conflict between Baal and Yam as a struggle for order and shows that chaos is overcome through divine military strength. The Hebrew creation story makes a decisive break from highlighting militaristic strength and violence as driving forces of the gods. Rather, the projection of God that the Bible presents in Genesis is a God of creation from nothing out of divine pleasure (God likes creating!). Humans are created in God's likeness and image. The world is good, as is light and land and all the animals. The biblical story presents a completely other imaginative reach for a description of God and seeks to plumb the depths of the conundrum of describing the relationship between God and humans.[9]

Mary Doria Russell, in her novel *Children of God*, describes God as one who walks among "the benighted creatures He just can't seem to give up on. There is a glorious looniness to it—the magnificent eternal gesture of salvation in the face of perennial, thick-headed human inanity. I like that in a God."[10]

While finding a comprehensive and final description for God in the Bible is impossible, it does suggest a compelling description of the underlying convictions that the biblical authors kept returning to again and again, and that is that God creates, forgives, redeems, saves, liberates, restores, judges injustice, and holds us accountable for the injustice. God is beyond human comprehension and yet is the spiritual force that holds things together. The

---

9. Heschel, *Man's Quest for God*; Heschel, *God in Search of Man*.
10. Russell, *Children of God*, 264.

questions raised by the first seekers are the same as contemporary seekers. This motivates me and shapes my life. I can use my imagination too. My curiosity is raised. How does my conception of God shape how I am living now?

Yes, this incomplete description of God leaves lots of holes, and it doesn't answer all the questions one might have. Yet, this more open, imaginative, and honest way of confronting the question of God seems right to me. Narrowing the options and emphasizing God as ultimate judge separating sinners from saints is limiting and not very helpful. But I have given up trying to make all things fit. You start with what makes sense, and what motivates, encourages, and increases curiosity, and let the other things go. Continue to circle the mystery of how it all fits for you. While there has always been a historic and human desire for uniformity and consistency, the reality is that the imaginative yearning to know more propels us into the creative process of describing the indescribable.

WHAT HAPPENS WHEN YOU DIE?

I found it interesting that the group didn't seem all that concerned about the question of the afterlife. They were much more interested in talking about how they were to live their lives in the here and now. However, their comments about growing up in churches that stressed God's judgment, sin, and damnation indicated that curiosity about what happens when you die was present, if only indirectly expressed. Perhaps if I had asked, "What do you think happens after you die?" members of the conversation group would have had a variety of answers. However, it didn't come up as a high-priority concern. I suspect that as one ages, the issue of what happens after death becomes more important. Nevertheless, the Pew study on the religious landscape indicated that a majority of young people of whatever self-identified religious affiliation or non-affiliation expressed their belief in an afterlife that includes heaven and/or hell (70 percent).[11]

Certainly, traditional Christianity stresses a continued life after death—at least spiritual or conscious existence after death. In fact, for many traditional believers the goal of life on earth and the reason you become a Christian is to get into the heavenly afterlife and avoid hell. Throughout the Bible there are references, descriptions, promises of a place, a house, a "mansion with many rooms" where a person goes to after death. Popular imagination portrays heaven as a paradise of angels, golden streets, virgins, and eternal bliss while hell is a place of fire and brimstone where there is crying and "gnashing of teeth." Islam also emphasizes a final judgment and a place where the righteous and unrighteous go. There is less of an emphasis in biblical Judaism about an afterlife. In Ps 1 the wicked don't go to hell, they "are like chaff that the wind drives away"(verse 4; NRSVUE). All who die go to Sheol, the place of the dead. Those who die cannot praise God (Pss 6:5, 30:9, 115:17). By the first century, different Jewish groups believed different things about life after death (Matt 22:22–33).

Today, there have been descriptions of individuals who have "died" and experienced an awareness of light, of a hovering where they saw their own bodies, of seeing Jesus or loved ones.[12] I will never forget visiting a woman who I had known for many years who was near death. Before entering her room, her nurse said, "She is not going to recognize you. She is hallucinating." I entered the room, greeted her, and asked her how she was. She responded by describing herself in a long, two-tiered hallway with many doors. She described herself as walking down the hall and deceased family members and friends coming out of the doors to greet her.

There was a young man who was dying of AIDS. He was gay. It was the 1990s when HIV/AIDS was ravaging the gay community, and many who were afflicted were ostracized from their family and churches. As I got to know this man, he shared that he was told he was going to hell, that he was "anathema" to God,

11. Smith et al., "Religious Landscape Study."
12. See Greyson, *After*.

an abomination, and would be forever cut off. The pastor of his church refused to visit him. A friend of this man's mother asked if I would go visit.

As we talked, I asked him about how he was facing death. He smiled and said, "I saw all my friends in heaven. They were reaching down and telling me to hurry up and join the party." I still get chills as I remember that interaction. I don't want to dismiss people's experience. In fact, I want to celebrate and learn from them, having my own experience and imagination challenged and stretched.

Among religious people the belief in an afterlife as a place or realm of consciousness with some sort of judgment that separates the good from the bad is generally accepted. Many argue that without the promise (or threat) of an afterlife, there is little incentive to control human impulses; there is no goal to reach for. I suspect that there is overwhelming agreement that if there is a hell, then Adolf Hitler should be there, and if there is a heaven, then Mother Teresa should be there. But between the obvious evil and celebrated good, there is a vast space for conversation and curiosity.

The goal of this chapter is not to seek to answer the unanswerable. Rather, it is to invite deeper reflection and to open conversation. Personally, I don't think you have to believe in life after death, or in heaven and hell, to be a Christian. No, I don't think there has to be heaven and hell to motivate behavior. As I age and death draws closer, perhaps I will change my mind. We shall see.

My mother, who will soon turn ninety-seven, has been a faithful Christian since her childhood. Over the past few years, she has shared with me that she doesn't really believe in a life after death anymore. Rather, for her it is a matter of where her life energy goes. She takes some comfort in the possibility that her energy will be added to the universal energy in the eternal physics of presence. Humans are, after all, made up of the same minerals and substance as everything else; we are all stardust. She has come to doubt hell as a real place—heaven too. Over time she has jettisoned, let go of, so many of the standard Christian beliefs that she had been taught. However, she hasn't given up on her Christian faith.

My mother is living the question of mortality; it is very present to her. It is a day-to-day stepping into the reality that she doesn't have too many days left. She admits to the uncertainty and fear that creeps in now and again. She yearns to know with certainty. Yet, she realizes that she can't find certainty with any certainty. But she rises each morning, washes, dresses well, heads to her pottery class, eats with her friends, goes to church, and lives a rich and full life. Does it matter that she doesn't know if she believes the traditional answers? Is she less of a Christian?

When serving the church where the young people asked who made God, I had a conversation with a woman who was near death. Finding a deeper curiosity with her than I did with the kids, I asked her, "What is dying like?" Her answer I will never forget. She looked at me and said, "It's awesome. I just have to whisper." I am particularly moved by the response of this woman who was near death. I'm not sure I understand it, but I feel it! I hope I "just have to whisper" as I face the awesomeness of the passage. But who knows.

I knew a man who was a Christian who knew the precise moment when he "gave his life to Christ." He lived with such confidence and purpose. Yet, in the days before his death, he was terrified that he wouldn't go to heaven.

What draws me into a deeper place is realizing that people of great wisdom, shaped by the experience of living, offer a variety of perspective that seem to open the mystery rather than shutting it down with pat answers. Likewise, I understand and respect those whose life have been so filled with misery that to imagine and hope for a life after death where there is justice, rest, and reward for the righteous and punishment for the unrighteous keeps them moving; it makes the struggle of daily living even worth it. This belief is certainly supported by many passages found in the Hebrew Scriptures and the New Testament. But is there a right or wrong answer to all these questions?

Personally, my imagination has always been drawn to the idea of purgatory, which is a teaching of Roman Catholic theology. Purgatory is a place where a soul goes after dying and before moving on. In Bruce Marshall's lovely book *All Glorious Within*, the main character, Father Smith, is musing, "Of course, there was purgatory, wherein the weak and the worldly were made clean, because even the best of men couldn't hope to go clod-hopping straight into God's presence after spending a lifetime talking about umbrellas and colds in the head."[13] If there is an afterlife I wonder if any of us are ready for the full blast of whatever. Perhaps we need to go through a kind of process of preparation, a cleansing of sorts.

The scene in the final book and movie of the *Harry Potter* series is where Harry is apparently killed by Voldemort, who is also apparently killed in the confrontation. Harry wakes up in a white place, a train station of sorts. Dumbledore appears and suggests that Harry has a choice of moving on or going back. Present too, under a bench, wrapped in white linen, is a swaddled figure without features that turns out to be Voldemort—his damaged, hate-filled life has ultimately limited him. Of course, this scene arises out of J. K. Rowling's fictional imagination, but that is not to say that there is not something to it.[14]

At this stage in my life, I want to hold these questions loosely. If, after I die, I am conscious of a next stage where I am beyond space and time, among the ancestors and spirits, having all my questions answered, being with God, seeing Jesus, then it will be the most wonderful surprise one can imagine. Actually, I like to imagine this. However, if after I die I become the compost for a tree, or my body or my ashes rest wherever they are placed, I won't know, so I won't care.

As far as heaven and hell. I have come to trust that God loves me, and so I don't have to fear the future. I trust in a spirit of love that overcomes everything, so I don't think I have to have the right answers or the proper confession. The descriptions of heaven and hell in the Bible are not meant to be taken literally but rather to express the imaginative yearnings of those individuals and communities who were led to fathom the unfathomable.

---

13. Marshall, *All Glorious Within*, 8.
14. Rowling, *Deathly Hallows*, 703–8.

While many Christians would disagree with me, I don't think the deepest questions of faith should leave us faced with a final binary choice. That simply doesn't make sense to me. And I don't think this is what the Bible teaches or what Jesus revealed. But more on that later.

One of the questions raised in the group that most intrigued me was, "What difference does any of this make? So what?" Indeed, does any of this matter? If the questions of life after death, heaven and hell, invite you to consider how you are living now, what is most important to you and what difference that makes, how you want to be remembered after you die, and what kind of example you want to leave your children, then it matters quite a bit, I think.

Any of the questions that open up possibilities, make you wonder, engage your imagination, and increase your creativity are all for the good. Personally, I am open to waiting and seeing . . . what else is there. Yes, *hoping* but not *needing* to know for certain, as I continue to live my present life to the full. I don't need heaven and hell to direct my choices, but I like to imagine an expansive future for me and those I love.

CHAPTER 6

Who Is Jesus?

Oh pale Galilean you have taken the spice out of life.
—ALGERNON CHARLES SWINBURNE, "HYMN TO PROSERPINE"

For Christ plays in ten thousand places,
Lovely in limbs, and lovely in eyes not his
To the Father through the features of men's faces.
—GERARD MANLEY HOPKINS, "AS KINGFISHERS CATCH FIRE"

SEVERAL PEOPLE IN THE small group asked, "Was Jesus a real person, or just made up?" "Was Jesus a Christian?" "Was Jesus really a white guy?" "What part of Jesus was divine and what part was human?" "Did Jesus really rise from the dead?" Unpacking the questions that surround this central figure is of primary importance.

Algernon Swinburne was a British poet and playwright who lived during the Victorian era. He was a vocal critic of the conservative nature of his time. The epigraph at beginning of this chapter indicates his reaction to the way Jesus was portrayed. Jesus was seen as the representative of a hierarchical, monarchical, imperial church where people knew their place and kept to it. Great Britain "ruled the waves," bringing its form of Christianity to the world. Swinburne takes for granted that Jesus was a "white man," calling him a "pale Galilean."

Through the ages Jesus has been portrayed as the conquering hero leading armies into battle, the meek and mild hippie, the muscle-ripped gym rat of the "no pain, no gain" T-shirt, the social activist, and the counter-culture, go-back-to-nature guru. Disastrously, in my opinion, modern white Christian nationalists are using Jesus to promote a takeover of the American government. No wonder so many want nothing to do with Jesus and the institution and culture that promote him.

Every culture and era have used Jesus to represent their culture, their norms, their times. Jesus as a white European still, embarrassingly, dominates the scene. Thankfully artists over the past one hundred years have stretched and corrected this narrow depiction of Jesus. Truly, Jesus "plays in ten thousand places . . . through the feature of men's faces."

What is true in all of this is that people see in Jesus what they want to see. This goes for me too. In some ways, I think it is a good thing that we can't definitively say who Jesus was and what his words and actions definitively meant. As we explore the questions around Jesus, it is good to keep this in mind. Jesus has always been and will always be a mysterious figure. We really don't know much about him, and yet each generation continues to ask the question, "Who is this guy who has had such an impact on world history?" There is no debate: Jesus is up there with Moses, Mohammed, and the Buddha as the GOAT, as far as religious change agents go.

Here are the facts: we really don't have much to go on to write a historic biography of Jesus.[1] He was born in Palestine when it was under Roman occupation. We know little or nothing about his childhood and young adult years. He was a teacher and miracle worker. He was crucified (a form of Roman capital punishment). He was reported, by his followers, to have come back to life.

---

1. See Aslan, *Zealot*; Pagels, *Miracles and Wonder*.

Who Is Jesus?

The four Gospels are our main primary sources: Matthew, Mark, Luke, and John. However, they are clearly theological interpretations of the significance of Jesus' adult life, indeed of his last year (Matthew, Mark, and Luke) or years (John).

The word "gospel" is a clue that the writers are not writing objective biographies of Jesus. Gospel is an English translation of the Greek word *evangelion*, which means "good news." So, the Gospels are, by definition, narratives proclaiming and promoting a certain "take" on Jesus.

If you read the Gospels carefully, you notice that only Matthew and Luke mention anything about the birth of Jesus (and they don't agree on several details). Only Luke adds something about Jesus' youth.

The Gospel of John also starts his narrative with the baptism of the adult Jesus, but John adds a theological prologue about Jesus being one with the creator as the "word" from the beginning of time. This is clearly not a provable historical insight. The Gospel of Mark begins when Jesus is about thirty years old.

Of central importance to each of the Gospel writers is the final week of Jesus' life: his trial, crucifixion, and resurrection. The narrative of what is called the passion of Jesus takes up from 25 percent to 33 percent of each Gospel. It is the interpretive lens through which the rest of the Gospel is read.

Many writers and poets through the ages have noticed that little or nothing is known about the childhood years of Jesus and tried to fill in the gaps. As mentioned, only the Gospel of Luke adds a story about a preteen Jesus. However, there were many stories circulating in the late first century and second century about Jesus' youth that didn't make the Bible. My favorite one tells the story of Jesus getting angry at a friend and zapping him with a spell right out of *Harry Potter*. The friend is killed. Mary, the mother of Jesus, forces her son to heal the stricken boy, which Jesus does.[2]

More recently the singer-songwriter John Prine wrote a song titled, "Jesus: The Missing Years."[3] Prine's verses about Jesus are not

---

2. See Mattison's translation of Inf. Gos. Thom. 3.3, 4.1–2.
3. Prine, "Jesus."

historical but are playful, and make you wonder. Taking up after Luke's story about Jesus as a twelve-year-old, Prine sings that Jesus leaves West Bethlehem and travels to France, Spain, and Rome, where he marries an Irish bride. When asked what he wants to be when he grows up, Prine's Jesus responds, "God."

Of course, Prine's song is parody and not to be taken as any kind of serious history. However, in his playful way Prine asks what authors—both believers and nonbelievers—have asked through the centuries: Who was Jesus? Why don't we know more about him? Each generation of "contemporary peers" is invited to refashion and reinterpret the story of Jesus.

Other than the four Gospels and a few stories in the books that didn't make the Bible (and John Prine), there is a brief passage in the writings of the first-century Jewish historian Josephus that names a small group of people who follow someone called "Christ."[4]

The other thing about the Gospels is that they were all written thirty to seventy years after Jesus' death at the hands of the Romans. Certainly, the four Gospels are important sources for trying to write a biography of Jesus. But the Gospels are not biographies. The Gospel writers are not trying to be objective, scientific, critical historians. They are proclaiming Jesus as the resurrected Son of God. This proclamation is of foundational importance to historical Christianity but hardly contains facts that can be proven.

Yet the Gospels remain. They are the primary interpretive source for who Jesus was and what Jesus did and what his life and death (and resurrection) mean. Within their pages are jewels of wisdom, some that we can, with a pretty high sense of accuracy conclude, reflect as close as we can get to the actual words of Jesus.

As we explore the questions encircling Jesus, I will use Mark's Gospel as the base since it is the earliest of the Gospels. However, I will then reference Matthew, Luke, and John to build the supports. But don't just take my word for it, or my methodology for granted. The point of this book is to invite you to love and honor

---

4. There is a reference to the "Christ" in Josephus, *Antiquities* 18.3.3; then in 20.9.1, Josephus refers to "James, the brother of Jesus who was called Christ."

the questions that are raised for you as you read the texts and work it out for yourself—or better, in community with others.

Start with Mark's Gospel. Mark's is the earliest of the four Gospels, likely written sometime in the sixties of the first century of the common era. This would mean that Mark was writing about thirty years after Jesus' death.

Read through Mark in one sitting. It is very short. If you read with a literary eye, you will notice that the action and tension builds, unwinds, and then builds again to a crescendo during the final week of Jesus' life. Rather startling is the report of Easter morning. Women followers of Jesus come to the tomb, and they find it empty. An unknown young man in a white robe tells them that Jesus has risen. What do the women do with this Easter good news? They run away terrified and say nothing to anyone.

You will notice in some Bibles that there are several endings to Mark. This clearly indicates that the first readers of Mark weren't satisfied with the ending at Mark 16:8. They had questions, so they answered them by writing their own endings or appropriating the work of others. Once again, questions drive people to come up with a multitude of answers.

Having briefly described the structure of Mark's Gospel, let's return to Jesus. As you read the Gospel of Mark, what do you notice about Jesus? He was a mysterious figure who one day appeared by the Jordan river as part of a large crowd drawn to the charismatic figure that we know as John the Baptist. Historians argue about Jesus' relationship with John: Was Jesus a disciple of John? Had Jesus spent time in the desert with his teacher? No one can say anything definitive, and this question is far beyond the bounds of this book. It is, however, a very interesting rabbit hole to climb down. I encourage you to follow it in your spare time, as you build up a capacity to sort the sources and sieve the multitude of questions.

You pick up clues as you read Mark that Jesus was misunderstood. Throughout the Gospel people are wondering who this guy is. Jesus asks his disciples, "Who do you say that I am?" (Mark 8:29). I have come to think that Jesus was not only asking the question as a kind of test to see if his followers had the right answer, but he was also asking the question because Jesus himself wasn't sure who he was and what his calling was. I like to think that his own identity was developing as he lived, as he encountered others. Isn't that how we experience our own lives? Yes, my interpretation is not the standard one. In fact, some may think it flat out wrong. You might as well.

Traditionally, most Christians have believed that Jesus knew that he was the Son of God and had a pretty firm grasp of his purpose and mission. This proclamation is shaped primarily from a reading of John's Gospel, who has a very different take on Jesus. Yet, I remain convinced that reading Mark and the other three Gospels with a questioning mind and heart, feeling your way through the Gospels, and paying attention to the tensions in the text opens a variety of ways to interpret Jesus that continue to challenge, compel, and may reveal deep truths. In fact, I have come to believe that people who pick up the Bible without former or formal training, without—yes—the indoctrination of well-meaning Sunday School teachers and preachers, may be better able to get to the heart of the matter.

Jesus was a mystic of sorts. He claimed a relationship with God, who Jesus called *Abba*, an Aramaic word for "father." Jesus is reported to have heard God call him "my beloved son." Jesus spent a period of days in the desert listening and struggling to come to terms with his own vocation. His experience in the wilderness, which is described in more detail in Matthew and Luke's Gospel, is described as a struggle with demonic powers. The essential questions that are raised concern what Jesus' mission is, what kind of power he possesses, and how he uses it. According to Mark, Jesus returns from his desert experience with a proclamation: "Now is the time! Here comes God's kingdom!" (Mark 1:15).

What does this mean? Later in Mark, Jesus is talking to a Jewish religious leader. They are having a conversation about the laws and commandments, the things that one must do to be a good and righteous believer.

If you will allow me a short detour.

Later in the book we will get to the question of the relationship of Christianity to Judaism and to other religions. For now, it is important to remind you that Jesus was Jewish. There were a variety of Jewish sects then and now that have varying interpretations—just as modern-day Christians have—about what one is supposed to believe and do. Jesus' own faith understanding was shaped by the words of the classic prophets (Isaiah, to name the most important) who declared that God demanded justice for the poor, equity for the marginalized, and release of the captive. Isaiah and Jesus despised religious hypocrisy and self-righteousness. Hypocrisy and self-righteousness are still two of the most noted reasons why people leave the church!

Furthermore, Jesus was a reformer. He wanted to do away with all the rules and obligations that got in the way of the essentials of faith and life.

Now returning to Jesus' dialogue with the Jewish scholar (scribe). The scribe asks Jesus, "Which commandment is the most important of all?" (Mark 12:28). Jesus responds with the traditional Jewish words to love God and love your neighbor. The scribe agrees that to love God and love neighbor is more important than anything else. Jesus answers, "You aren't far from God's kingdom" (Mark 12:34).

The "kingdom of God" (or in Matthew's Gospel, the "kingdom of heaven") is not beyond time, space, or place; it is a present lived opportunity. Where people are seeking to love God and love others, they are close to the kingdom—living the kingdom in the here and now.

I believe that one of the most harmful fallacies that has developed in Christianity through the ages is this conviction that the most important aspect of Jesus' teaching had to do with getting into heaven. Rather, Jesus is clear that faith is about how you treat others, and how one seeks to find meaning with the higher power. In Matthew's Gospel, Jesus proclaims that we will only be judged by how we treat the hungry, the naked, the stranger, the prisoner (Matt 25). According to Luke, Jesus' message is summed up in his first sermon in Nazareth, up north in Galilee. There, Jesus lays it all out using the words of Isaiah the prophet: "The Spirit of the Lord is upon me, because the Lord has anointed me. He has sent me to preach good news to the poor, to proclaim release to the prisoners and recovery of sight to the blind, to liberate the oppressed, and to proclaim the year of the Lord's favor" (Luke 4:18–19). In these words Jesus again emphasizes action over articulated belief, human interaction rather than following a set of rules.

In Matthew's Gospel chapters 5 through 7, Jesus stresses the blessedness of the poor, those who mourn, the meek, those who hunger and thirst, the merciful, the pure in heart, and the peacemaker—in short, those who are just living and struggling, and those who pursue hospitality, nonjudgmental compassion, and peace.

There is nothing in these words from Jesus about what you are supposed to believe. Rather, it is an invitation to live justly and well—not to be concerned about wealth and status, power and prestige. Time and again, Jesus invites those judged unworthy, or unclean, to a table to share a meal. He often eats with religious leaders with whom he disagrees. Most of the time, those who spend time with Jesus are moved to change behavior rather than to make a new belief/faith statement. I find this very important. Jesus invited others to first belong to a community that behaved in a particular way. Only as one lived and practiced this new kingdom life did their words change and their understanding and belief develop.

Jesus, like John the Baptist before him, uses the word "repent." Traditional Christianity has too often used this word like a bludgeon on hurting and broken people. "Repent" is traditionally used to emphasize the sinfulness of each person. The traditional formula follows something like this: driven to despair by the fear of judgment and eternal damnation, a person realizes their need for a change of course, repents, and receives salvation. They are on a new path, their life forever changed; they are now "fit" for heaven.

I have known many people for whom this process describes their experience. I can't dismiss this out of hand. Too many have had their life changed for the better to simply throw out this definition of "repent."

Yet this narrow definition doesn't fit everyone. Some churches seem particularly focused on certain groups of people who need repentance more than others. Too many people have been driven by fear, guilt, and obligation by some churches and some Christians. This doesn't sound very Jesus-like to me. Furthermore, there is a tendency to use the word "repent" as a one-time event, instead of a constant course correction through life.

There is another definition of "repent" which I have always found helpful, freeing, and frankly closer to what I think Jesus really meant. The Greek word for "repent" is *metanoia*, which more literally means a "change of mind." A mentor of mine, the late Reverend Dr. Herb Meza, once preached a sermon about repentance that I will never forget, and it literally changed my mind about the word. Dr. Meza said that the best way to define the word "repent" is, "Get a new mind for a new age!" Jesus wasn't telling the people to feel guilty and horrible so that they could repent and be on the fast track to heaven. Rather, Jesus was bringing in a new age. One of equity and inclusion, welcoming the stranger, sharing the bounty so that everyone had something. This is the point of Jesus' feeding miracle, isn't it? When we share, there is more than enough. This new age which was, to Jesus, the coming of the kingdom of God was not in the future; it was as near as our ability to live it.

As you wonder about the central message of Jesus, consider his words about the kingdom of God. What would that look like for you? What would our country look like if we truly shaped our politics by what Jesus said about the kingdom of God? How would the geopolitical reality of the world change?

Jesus is reported to have been a miracle worker who healed people and cast out demons. In these actions too, Jesus shows what he means by the kingdom of God drawing near. In the first century, as in our day, there were individuals reported to have had powers to heal and to cast out demons. Were some of the maladies described in the Gospels as demon possession really something more common, like schizophrenia or other kinds of mental illnesses? Perhaps, but apparently whatever the diagnosis, Jesus was recognized as a healer. You will have to wrestle with whether or not this is important to you. Yet the stories again emphasize that Jesus didn't discriminate—he healed individuals of varying status and social standing. If you read the healing stories, Jesus was always touching or being touched by those who were thought to be unclean by the culture of the day: menstruating women, lepers, beggars, and Samaritans are named as "others" in the biblical texts. Jesus consistently invited those people who were told they didn't belong to the table.

In my reading, most of the time there was no transaction; Jesus invited folks just as they were. Outsiders became insiders. Those who were deemed "unclean" by the religious authorities were made "clean" and invited in.

The American poet Edwin Markham, I think, gets to the heart of the message of Jesus in his poem "Outwitted," written in 1899.

> He drew a circle that shut me out—
> Heretic, rebel, a thing to flout.
> But Love and I had the wit to win:
> We drew a circle and took him in![5]

Most of the time Jesus didn't even ask anyone to change. It is true that the stories indicate that great changes often occurred in people's lives (money given away, becoming a disciple), but the change came in response to being accepted, included, healed; it had little or nothing to do with a change in what one said they believed or didn't. Jesus wasn't transactional. Jesus' miracles indicate the expansion of inclusion and an invitation to belong to a new kind of community.

Jesus believed that this is what God wanted—not a building up of new barriers, writing new rules, burdening people with new expectations, driving people to despair and guilt, but rather a pulling down of requirements and expectations, taking down the walls of separation and division. To me, this is still good news that we need to hear and live by.

Not too long ago I heard a preacher declare that Jesus raised the bar for holy living; one had to live up to the call of Jesus. The implication was that most of us don't, and we shouldn't feel good about that; all the more reason to repent. When I heard these words, I asked myself, "Didn't Jesus break every barrier down? He didn't raise the bar; he threw the bar away!"

---

5. Markham, "Outwitted," in Untermeyer, *Modern American Poetry*, 48.

Who Is Jesus?

There are stories about Jesus casting demons out of people and in one case directing the demons to enter a herd of pigs. In the story found in Mark 5, Jesus asks the demon to identify itself, and it responds, "Legion is my name, because we are many" (Mark 5:9). As John Dominic Crossan[6] has pointed out, the name Legion is significant. A legion was the largest military unit of the imperial Roman army. Each legion consisted of almost five thousand soldiers. In casting out the demon, Jesus is making quite the political statement. The power of Jesus challenges the might of the Roman empire. Jesus' kingdom ethic is held up as an alternative to the political/military/industrial complex!

This is a subtle point but one worth considering when you are thinking about who Jesus was and who Jesus may be for us today. The way of Jesus, the way of the kingdom of God, is a challenge, an alternative to the political and military powers. This alternative, subversive way of Jesus is hinted at in the Christmas story. Read the opening verses of the second chapter in Luke's Gospel. Luke names Emperor Augustus, who was also reported to have had a miraculous birth.[7] Luke then describes the miraculous birth of Jesus—who, like Augustus, comes from a royal lineage (King David). The angels recognize the significance of what is going on: the way of Jesus as the subversive alternative to the way of imperial power. Perhaps the way of Jesus continues to be a subversive alternative to the way of our present politics and our continuing imperial and dominating culture. When you read with curiosity, all sorts of things start arising. Pay attention! When you read the Gospels, you will come to find so much more that is interesting and challenging. There are many wonderful scholarly guidebooks that can lead you deeper.

However, by yourself or with a small group, you can begin to explore. You will notice that the miracles of Matthew, Mark, and Luke are different from the miracles in John's Gospel. In John's Gospel, miracles are called "signs." You will see that the chronology

---

6. See Crossan, *Historical Jesus*, 314–15; see also Crossan, *God and Empire*.

7. Suetonius was a Roman historian. He writes of Augustus's divine birth in *Augustus* 2.94. The story of Augustus's birth was found in Roman propaganda of the first century.

of John's Gospel is not the same as the first three Gospels. Jesus, in the fourth Gospel, sounds different. John's take is certainly an alternative one. I hope that you find these differences exciting and inviting. Hold it all loosely; don't try to force things together. Always ask, "What do I notice? What do I think the author is saying?" "How would I answer the question, 'Who is Jesus?'" Jesus healed, performed miracles, and taught. Everything he said and did pointed to, revealed, his understanding of the kingdom of God.

As you explore the text, be sure to look at Luke 4:14–19 and Compare Matt 5:1–20 with Luke 6:20–26 (Jesus' Sermon on the Mount). Read Luke 1:46–55 (Mary's song, known as the "Magnificat"). Lean into the Lord's Prayer found in Matt 6:9–13 and Luke 11:2–4. In that well known prayer, recited every Sunday in almost every church in the world, you are as near to the real words of Jesus that you may get. Notice that we are praying for God's will (desire, intention) to be done on earth so that it reflects the way God would want it. And how does God want the world to be, to reflect the heavenly norm? Sharing daily bread, forgiving debt, not falling into the false paths (temptations) of life are identified as central. Again, the emphasis is on action, not dogma.

Take time to think about the temptations we fall into as individuals and as a culture. Expand your notion of temptation beyond sex, drugs, and candy. This prayer is not just about you. It is a prayer both for the community and for the world. Perhaps the message of Jesus is more focused on the way of the community and how we live together rather than on individual behavior.

From the exercise of reading these passages, I think you will see a message that is far more radical than we have been led to think. You may have wonderful memories of your Sunday school teacher telling you about Jesus meek and mild. Yes, Jesus welcomed children and directed us to chill out a bit and consider the lilies of the field and the sparrows of the air. And for a full, contented, richer life we should do these more contemplative practices. However, Jesus wasn't killed for encouraging people to slow down and notice flowers. Jesus was talking about and living an earthly nonviolent overthrow of the status quo, calling us all to live in a heavenly community in the here and now. How does that feel? Does it correspond to your reading of the Bible?

Jesus taught in a particular fashion called the parable. There are many books about the parables.[8] For our purpose, it is enough to say that Jesus used everyday situations (fields and farms, parties, kitchens, broken-hearted fathers, narcissistic rich folk, harsh farmers, wasteful people) to reveal aspects of the kingdom of God. Jesus used similes and metaphors. Metaphorical language demands the reader to be open and think big. Often a parable will begin with the words, "With what shall I compare the kingdom?" or, "The kingdom of heaven is like . . ." Readers have misinterpreted the parables thinking that there is a single meaning to be found in each one. Scholars through the years have come up with varying interpretations. All well and good. However, the purpose of the parable was to confuse and to agitate or stir things up like a washing machine does to clothes (Mark 4:10–12).

I believe Jesus used the parable style to make his listeners feel uncomfortable and rattled. My guess is that the initial response from those who were in the crowd when Jesus told his parables was, "What?" Is the mustard seed (Matthew 13:31–32) a sign of the kingdom because it is small or because it is a weed that no farmer would want to grow in his field? Maybe both and maybe something more.

After reading a parable, reflect on how it makes you feel, rather than trying to figure it out. Yes, there are a few parables where an explanation is given, purportedly by Jesus himself. I am not alone in thinking that the few explanations of the parables are not from Jesus himself but rather from later interpreters trying to make sense of the confusion. Like you and me, the early Christians too were agitated and confused and wanted to give answers rather than invite folks to hold the discomfort.

This isn't the book to go deep into textual criticism. There are many learned scholars who can take you there. Suffice to say, in my opinion Jesus raised more questions and invited more questions than he gave answers. It goes against our grain as humans, but the words of Thomas Merton remind me that the longer you can stay

---

8. I recommend Levine, *Short Stories by Jesus*.

in the tension, the better. Jesus invited us into the tension of wondering. When you give up certainty, there is space for openness and fascination and letting a lot of things go. You live paying attention to the tensions and complexities, like a multiverse of possibilities. I believe this is the start of wisdom and deeper knowledge. Some may find my answer frustrating, but it is where I am.

WHY IS THE CROSS IMPORTANT AND DID JESUS REALLY RISE FROM THE DEAD?

As noted above, all the gospels report that Jesus died on a cross. "Why does the cross matter?" "Why is being "saved" important?" These two questions interested as well as confused several members of the group.

Today the cross is seen on highway hillsides and has become a popular fashion accessory. As Misty White Sidell notes in her New York Times article, the cross is "seen on influencers, pop stars and White House staff, cross necklaces are popping up everywhere."[9] The popular singer Chappell Roan, the White House press secretary Karoline Leavitt, and Attorney General Pam Bondi all wear cross necklaces. Sidell interviewed Sage Mills, a student at the University of Oklahoma. Ms. Mills said "seeing women in government like Ms. Leavitt and Ms. Bondi wear their own crosses makes me feel good. It makes me feel like God is the important thing for people that are governing our world."[10]

The cross as a sign of pop status, political influence and power is a far cry from its original significance.

Death by crucifixion on a cross was a humiliating and brutal means of Roman capital punishment. For example, in 73 B.C.E thousands of rebels were executed in this manner. It was reported that crosses lined the Appian Way in Italy serving as a deterrent against future uprisings.[11] That Jesus was executed on a cross by

---

9. Misty White Sidel "A Hot Accessory at the Intersection of Faith and Culture" New York Times April 29, 2025.
10. Sidel, "A Hot Accessory"
11. Appian's Civil War 1.120

the Romans indicates that they saw him as, at very least, a potential political revolutionary. The word was that Jesus was being called the next "King of the Jews."

The earliest Christians knew of the shame of the cross (Hebrews 12). To be crucified on a cross was to die a shameful, brutal, agonizing death. Perhaps because of the shameful association of the cross, the fish, the circle and the anchor predated the cross as the main symbols of early Christian faith.

The cross became a symbol, for Christians, of the sacrificial death of Jesus who took away the "sins of the world." I think it is important to note, contrary to the understanding of many Christians, that this claim is broadly collective, dare I say, universal rather than a promise for individuals only.

The cross signifies the vertical connection between heaven and earth, the divine and human as well as the horizontal connection binding all of humanity together. The cross represents the restorative power of divine love for all creation. The cross is a sign of sacrifice, love and repair. As Jesus lay down his life for his friends, so too are we to put others before self. The cross represents all the under-represented, the marginalized, and the oppressed. The cross reminds us that God stands with the poor, the hungry, the dispossessed, the prisoner, and the immigrant. The cross stands in defiant judgement of abusive power.

The cross did not become the primary symbol of the faith until the 4th century. Some historians say that this coincided with the conversation of the emperor Constantine in 312 CE at Milvian Bridge, when it is reported that the emperor had a dream in which he saw the cross and received the message: "In hoc signo vinces" ("In this sign, you will conquer").

As Christianity became the religion of the Roman Empire the cross became a sign of military conquest. No longer a sign of humiliation and agony but rather a sign of retribution and domination. The cross led the crusades, and the pogroms, and the inquisition. The cross became a sword.

Ultimately the cross is about love and forgiveness, Jesus showing the depth of God's acceptance of everyone. If you wear a cross, great! But first, think about what it means to you and what it holds you accountable for.

The cross has traditionally been the symbol to remind the wearer and to show the world that she, he or they have been "saved." But the words "save" and "salvation" are loaded and confusing. A member of the conversation group raised a very good question: "Saved from what and for what?"

Traditionally to be saved means that a person has come to understand their sinfulness and unworthiness. Repenting of their sins they turn to Jesus and accept him as their Lord and Savior. Being "saved" means that you have been made right with God. Furthermore, you will not go to hell when you die but rather to heaven. For many knowing the exact date and time of their salvation (when you accepted Jesus as your Savior) is of vital importance. According to this way of thinking, if you don't remember or are not sure when you were saved means that you probably aren't. In an earlier chapter I addressed the limited nature of this traditional understanding.

In the Hebrew scriptures words related to "save" and "salvation" come from the Hebrew root "Yasha" which can mean deliverance, rescue or help. In Exodus 14:13 God "saves" his people from the Egyptians. The word "savior" which has become one of the titles used for Jesus, is also found throughout the Hebrew scriptures (Isaiah 43:11 and Hosea 13:4).

This broader meaning of "save" provides a deeper and more nuanced understanding of the concept. Was there a time when you recall feeling lost but eventually found direction. Perhaps you struggled with addiction and found your way to safety through a 12-step program. Maybe you had an insight, found love, discovered a new way forward that literally "saved" you; brought you to a new way of looking at life and the world around you. I feel as if I have been "saved" many times throughout my life which encouraged me to engage more fully in my relationships, commit to justice, and to let things go that were keeping me from living a fuller more creative life.

Identifying with and being inspired by the cross and shaping your life by the example of Jesus, calls one into a life of service, sacrifice, compassion, imagination and love. The cross is still a challenge to the powers that be and a liberating (saving) symbol pointing to a transformative and creative way of being in the world.

Let's just get to perhaps the most pressing question that people have when they talk about Jesus. Did he really rise from the dead? The most that can be said with certainty is that some of the disciples of Jesus, having scattered after his death, came back together saying that they had experienced a personal interaction with him or a sense of his presence.

Paul of Tarsus, in the years immediately after the reported resurrection of Jesus, was charged with investigating the spread of this new Jesus movement and arresting the early believers. He too had an experience of Jesus on the road to Damascus that turned his life around. Paul spent the rest of his life proclaiming the truth of Jesus' resurrection and interpreting its significance to other early believers.

Some are convinced that Jesus' dead body actually and physically came back to life. For many, this profession is absolutely central to being a Christian. George, a friend, declared that if it could be proven that Jesus didn't rise from the dead, he would quit being a Christian. George is far from being alone in this belief.

But others see in the resurrection a metaphor that life and truth cannot be destroyed. Some would contend that the resurrection is less about what happened to Jesus and more about what happens to us when we shape our lives by the example of Jesus.

My experience leads me to believe that there are many people who circle the mystery of Jesus' life, death, and reported resurrection without certainty—uncomfortable asserting a statement that they are skeptical or not sure of. Rather than a binary choice of whether it happened or not, consider asking your questions and following your curiosity. I think that certainty can be or become a weight that hinders the seeker from going deeper into what the resurrection might mean to them. And besides, for me it is more important to live your life shaped by the example of Jesus, his teaching, and the power of resurrection hope, however you interpret it, than being certain about what happened after Jesus died.

What is a historic fact is that after Jesus died, the movement took off. A frightened group of his friends came back together—bound together in community, spreading a good news message of hospitality and forgiveness, calling people of every social status and station to form a beloved community. I think that especially in this present time of disruption, people of every age and station want to belong to this kind of community of hope, not based on doctrine and dogma but rather welcome.

There is great potential power in the community of the hopeful. It is a power to disrupt the status quo and to create something new. The words of Percy Bysshe Shelley in the last stanza of his poetic *Prometheus Unbound* (1820) speak to the creative resurrection power of those who gather to follow Jesus.

> To suffer woes which Hope thinks infinite;
> To forgive wrongs darker than death or night;
> To defy Power, which seems omnipotent;
> To love, and bear; to hope till Hope creates
> From its own wreck the thing it contemplates;
> Neither to change, nor faulter, nor repent;
> This, like thy glory, Titan, is to be
> Good, great and joyous, beautiful and free;
> This is alone Life, Joy, Empire, and Victory.[12]

My advice to those who wonder about the resurrection of Jesus is to go with what works for you at the present moment, keep an open mind, live the questions, and gather with other seekers who long for the unfolding journey of discovery.

Trying to put into words what you believe is an important exercise. It may change over time; in fact, it should. However, don't worry too much about trying to figure it all out. Frankly, I am more interested in how you live your life, what is important to you, what shapes your view of the world and your place in it.

For me, the words of Jesus reported in John's Gospel are a good place to start. Jesus is with his disciples on the night before

---

12. Shelly, *Prometheus Unbound*, act 4, lines 570–78.

he is to be executed. In John's account, Jesus is comforting his disciples who are frightened and confused about what is going to take place and what the execution of Jesus might mean for them. Jesus says to his disciples, "You know the way to the place I'm going" (John 14:4). Thomas, one of the disciples asks aloud, "What are you talking about?" (my paraphrase). Jesus answers Thomas, "I am the way, the truth, and the life. No one comes to the Father except through me. If you have really known me, you will also know the Father" (John 14:6–7).

This verse is one among several that is used by many Christians to indicate there is only one way to God and that is through Jesus. When used in such an exclusive manner, there is really no room for other religions, faith traditions, or perspectives. We will get into the issue of relationship of Christianity to other faith traditions in another chapter. For now, however, suffice it to say that this one verse had turned off and driven away many who are otherwise drawn to the community of the church. It doesn't feel right that good people who were born and raised in other cultures, faithful to their religious traditions, should be excluded from knowing God. I agree with them.

However, these words can be interpreted in a different way that is far less exclusive and actually invites us to take a closer look at Jesus. I think this verse invites us to a deeper reflection about three questions:

1. What is the way of Jesus and how do we follow it?
2. What is the truth that Jesus is revealing?
3. What is the life of Jesus and how do you and I live his life?

Seeking to answer those questions then points to the larger issue of how Jesus saw God and invites us to be curious about how we envision God.

In my opinion, the way, the truth, and the life of Jesus suggest a life that displays the following:

Nonviolence: You turn the other cheek and do not repay evil for evil. You pray for your enemies. I see nothing in Jesus that would glorify the military industrial complex or celebrate the ability to own semiautomatic weapons.

Inclusion of those who are seen as the "other": Today there are so many whose voices have been silenced and who are judged unworthy. It is the way that some demean the immigrant, those fleeing oppression, violence, and climate-caused drought. Although there has been much progress, the church is still the bastion of inhospitality to the LGBTQA+ community.

Self-sacrifice: Followers of Jesus do without and share what they have. They are generous and place a priority not upon selfish interest but the common good. Those who seek to walk the way, the truth, and the life of Jesus may face a negative reaction. As Veronica, a deeply faithful woman, once said, "Following Jesus is no walk through a rose garden." Following the way, the truth, and the life of Jesus may get you into trouble. After all, Jesus was arrested and put to death because the political powers and the religious leaders were afraid of the challenge to their authority that Jesus presented.

A mystic sense of reality: Followers of Jesus marvel at the wonder of everything, honoring creation and every person, recognizing that each individual is a beloved child of God. They seek an inward journey of spiritual discipline and walk an outer journey of service to others.

I love this example of what it means to follow the way, the truth, and the life of Jesus. An aide in a kindergarten class complained to the teacher that Charlie was a disruptive little boy. The aide was struggling with how to get past this dislike of this apparent little hellion. The teacher said to the aide, "Salute the Christ within Charlie." Yes! Salute the Christ within the little boy. Salute the Christ within everyone you meet. Salute the Christ within your enemy, your political opponent, the homeless man on the street, the immigrant mother struggling to find a place of safety for her and her children. Salute the Christ within yourself!

Jesus' way, truth, and life indicated that he believed that God was intimate; that God cared for the poor, the widow, and the orphan; and that the way God acted to support these people was through sharing, welcoming, questioning the reigning orthodoxy, imagining, and creating a new way of living. The followers of Jesus became the face, feet, and hands of God.

Jesus didn't come to start a church or a new religion. Rather, he started a movement that gave witness to what he believed God, the creator of all, wanted. This new movement was not built upon doctrine or dogma but rather the invitation to "come and see!"

"Come and see!" That is the invitation that Jesus gave to some disciples of John the Baptist in the first chapter of John (verses 35–39). Sensing that he is being followed, Jesus turns and says to those behind him, "What are you looking for?" And they said, "Rabbi [which means teacher], where are you staying?" This interchange is so meaningful for me. We are all looking for a place to land, to lay down our luggage (so to speak), to rest and feel secure. I think we are all looking for a sense of purpose and meaning—higher, perhaps even divine, meaning. In the small group of young adults, this yearning to be connected to something bigger (a big idea), to be "dissolved into something complete and great," as Willa Cather writers in My Ántonia,[13] was often expressed. Jesus still points to and represents this intersection along the continuum of time and eternity, of divinity and humanity, and of the inward quest and the outward expression. I believe that the question of those disciples is still resonating today: "Where are you staying?" Or, in other words, "Where can I find what I am looking for?" And Jesus' answer is, "Come and see." An invitation to a journey both of location and locomotion—never fully arriving but always a place at the table and a place to call home. Seeking to follow Jesus will lead to a lifetime of adventure. And, as Helen Keller once noted, "Life is either a daring adventure or nothing."[14]

---

13. Cather, *My Ántonia*, 18.
14. Keller, *Open Door*, 17.

Chapter 7

What Is the Bible and How Do You Read It?

There was something terrifying and fascinating about reading ancient texts, something that filled me with awe. Without moving I could ramble through worlds invisible and visible. I was in two places at once, a thousand places at once. I was with Adam at the beginning, barely awakened to a world streaming with light; with Moses in the Sinai under a flaming sky. I seized upon a phrase, a word, and distances vanished.

—Elie Wiesel, "All Rivers Run to the Sea"

The best arguments in the world won't change a single person's point of view.... The only thing that can do that is a good story. Good stories are a kind of benevolent Trojan horse. You let them in, and they add complication, allowing you to understand that sometimes a thing and its opposite are true at the same time.

—Ken Burns, *New York Times*, July 5, 2025

What Is the Bible and How Do You Read It?

"What is the Bible?" "How do you read it?" "Is it direct from God?" "What if science contradicts the Bible?" "Is the Bible true?" These are questions that have been asked throughout my years in ministry. They were also raised by the group gathered in the fellowship hall.

One day, several years ago, I was touring the Permian Basin Museum in Midland, Texas. I highly recommend the museum! My guide—a husband of my wife's cousin—is a Christian who believes in the inerrant literalism of the Bible. In other words, the Bible is correct in all matters of history and science.

Of greatest interest to me in the museum was the diorama of the Permian Basin from four billion years ago. According to the exhibit, the basin had once been an inland sea teeming with life that over time became the oil that runs the world. My in-law cousin guide, a university-educated man and a very successful businessman in the oil and gas industry, said as we stood looking at the diorama, "Well, of course the description of the age of the basin is wrong because the Bible teaches a seven-day creation." I was so stunned by that answer that I was speechless. I guess he thought that since I too was a Christian, and a pastor, I would of course agree. Perhaps he was testing me, prodding to see if I was *really* a person of faith, a "true" believer.

I reflect upon that memory with embarrassment and a bit of shame. Why didn't I ask, "Do you *really* believe that?" As I remember at the time, I didn't want to get into an argument—one that is so ideological in nature. So, I remained silent. But asking a question might have led to a deeper conversation, not an argument. I was afraid that if I responded with, "I believe the Genesis story is a rewriting of an earlier Ugaritic creation story," it would get uncomfortable. So, I remained silent. That diorama and my guide's remarks have stayed with me to this day. I didn't lead with curiosity.

How can anyone really think that the early writers of Scripture knew more than modern-day scientists? Well, if you believe without question that God directed the writing of the Bible and that God wouldn't lie, and therefore what the Bible says is factually true, then it makes a logical sense. But certainly, this is wrong—at least for me, anyway.

I was at a backyard barbecue outside of Seattle. My wife, Deanne, and I were there for a wedding. The evening before, friends and family members gathered. I found myself in a small group of men who were engaged in a lively conversation about whether or not the Bible supports the Second Amendment right to own firearms. They agreed that not only does the Bible support the unabated access to firearms in the United States, but they were also concerned about the faith of those who didn't agree with them. I raised what seemed like the obvious point, "But there is no mention of guns anywhere in the Bible." For me, the Bible encourages more of a concern for the common good and communal safety rather than one's individual right. But, of course, the Bible doesn't outright say that either.

I have lost count of the number of times I have discussed and argued with fellow Christians about what the Bible "teaches" and does not "teach" about homosexuality and gender-fluid identities. Many Christians look to a few verses that to me are very obscure, limited, and shaped by ancient culture and history to conclude with certainty that homosexuality is an aberration and anathema to God. I would counter that the Bible teaches that every person is precious in the sight of God. Jesus welcomed and continues to welcome everyone without regard to sexual preference or gender identity. My go-to text is found in Paul's letter to Galatians: "All of you who were baptized into Christ have clothed yourselves with Christ. There is neither Jew nor Greek; there is neither slave nor free; nor is there male and female, for you are all one in Christ Jesus" (Gal 3:27–28). While this text does not include the words "gay" or "straight," to me, Christianity is about breaking down boundaries; identities don't matter.

One of the most recent and frightful misuses (in my opinion) of the Bible is the support of the Seven Mountain Mandate, which seeks to control the seven spheres of influence: family, religion, education, media, arts and entertainment, business, and government. The goal of these Christian nationalists is to dominate and control life in America, making it conform to their interpretation of what the Bible demands and what God wants. I see nothing in this mandate that reflects the teaching of Jesus, Paul, or any of the first Christians up until Christianity became the imperial religion of Rome.

Many study the Bible to find guidance about marriage, the role of women in church, premarital sex, the necessity of corporal punishment of children, how to wage a moral war, and insight into how the world is going to end. The Bible for many Christians is a textbook for science and history. Remember my guide in the Permian Basin Museum who believed the Bible taught a seven-day creation.

While some read with literal precision, others interpret passages of Scripture more broadly. Many others, if not most, are lost in the haze of competing interpretations and place their Bibles on the shelf to collect dust, concluding that the Bible no longer has any relevance other than as a historic source reflecting outdated modes of thinking.

To me this use of the Bible as a precise answer book in all matters is misguided. It presumes a unifying authority that I don't think the Bible assumes. Furthermore, typically this more literal, exacting way of reading the Bible as an answer book for all of life's questions is grounded on a belief that God is involved in all these particularities, and therefore, if you want to please God, then you want to do what God spells out in the Bible. One's faith is directed to following the Bible with as much precision as possible. A corollary to this perspective often follows: *not* to use the Bible in this manner is an indication of not being a "real" Christian.

If the goal of faith is to get to heaven and the Bible is the answer book of the test of life, well then you had better do what the Bible says. In this understanding God has given his orders and commands in the Bible that one needs to follow to please God. God is keeping track and there will be a judgment, and everyone will be held accountable. This description of how to read the Bible is a perspective that many Christians hold. This way of reading the Bible is regarded with skepticism by many others, including myself.

I have found the Bible not only very useful but vitally important for helping me make life decisions. I, like my more conservative, literalist siblings, also want to follow the wisdom and teaching of the biblical authors. As I made clear in the previous chapter about Jesus, I want to follow as faithfully as possible what he taught. The prophetic calls for justice, mercy, and compassion for the poor that are trumpeted in Isaiah, Micah, Amos, and Jeremiah are guiding touchstones. I would even agree that God judges unrighteousness and injustice, both political and religious hypocrisy, that God gets angry when we do not show mercy or forgive as we have been forgiven. We are held accountable. However, I believe—because the Bible says it—that God's love and mercy trumps punishment and retribution. Psalm 30:5 proclaims, "[God's] anger lasts for only a second, but his favor lasts a lifetime." Of course, there are many verses that stress eternal judgment and punishment. But I don't think the final answer will be found by counting the number of verses that support one's opinion.

If you believe that ultimately mercy, love, and forgiveness win, then you interpret the more judgy verses in light of that perspective. Likewise, if you emphasize God's final judgment, righteous accountability, and the idea that only some get into heaven, well then you will interpret the gentler and forgiving passages in light of these passages. The fact that Christians disagree about how to interpret the Bible proves that there are multiple ways to come to any one conclusion at any one time.

In some ways I take the Bible literally and seek to follow it. I follow the Bible's call to "test the spirits," to "pray without ceasing," "to consider the lilies of the field," to be in awe of creation, and to "seek first the kingdom of God and its righteousness," trusting that everything else will unfold in time, falling into place. These biblical truths have guided me throughout my life and shaped my understanding of other passages. The biblical call to justice, hospitality, and generosity have shaped my ministry. These passages directed the church I served to become a sanctuary church. Members of the church protected an undocumented immigrant from Mexico for two years. The Bible's call for justice and mercy has called me to become involved in faith-based organizing, seeking to build power in order bring equity and justice to the underserved. The

Bible seems clear that we are to welcome the stranger and take care of the immigrant wanderer. I want to trust that "God works all things together for good for the ones who love God, for those who are called according to his purpose"(Rom 8:28).

Many passages of the Bible encourage me to make time to pray and discern, to stay open and trust that things will play out. Every moment is full of divine potential. There are no mistakes, just opportunities for growth and learning. In my years of reading the Bible, I have come to find that the underlying story, the thread that holds Genesis to Revelation together, is a profession that God creates, forgives, redeems, judges, liberates, and restores. I find this holy thread very helpful to me as I face life challenges and choices.

The Bible for me is also a fascinating collection of texts that invite us to deep wonder and questioning. We are called to circle the profound mysteries of life, adding our wisdom and insight to the wisdom and insight of the ages. The Bible is like some ancestral scrapbook revealing that the ancients were wondering about things that we wonder about. Experiences are shared, interpretations honed, arguments engaged. It is not about agreeing with every verse. Rather, it is about engaging and wrestling with the text. This is what I love about the quotation by Elie Wiesel at the beginning this chapter. His description of reading ancient texts as time travel—being present at creation, imagining what Adam was thinking, what inspired Moses, what drove Ruth, what called to Jesus, what made Mary cry out, "My soul magnifies the Lord!"—is exciting and challenging. It expands our thinking and offers perspective on our present lives.

The descriptive phrase of calling the Bible "the living word" is helpful to me—something that is alive, has life, continues to grow, expands, calls us into an imaginative relationship with the stories. Sometimes you have to cut dead branches off in order for new buds to form. Read the Bible with critical love. It is not just a rule book from the past or an ancient tome of wisdom or something set in stone never to be questioned.

Yes, there are rules and codes and commandments. Most of them most people agree with, such as murder is wrong, we should love our neighbor, creation is an awesome wonder that we should care for, we should give to the poor and speak truth to power. These are timeless truths shared by every culture and religious tradition. However, there are other rules, codes, and commandments that are so bound to the time, place, and culture of their first writing that it is harmful to follow them. Verses that limit the role of women and condemn queer people—to give but two examples—cannot be justified, and it is faithful to ignore such narrow conceits. Furthermore, once we get away from the general to the specific application of the rules, codes, and commandments, it gets dicey.

People of good faith interpret the Scripture in a variety of ways. I know many lifelong churchgoers and faithful Christians who are intimidated by those who can recite chapter and verse by heart and seem to have the "answer" all worked out. After a Bible study in which one person seemed to know every verse in the Bible and was confident that she had the definitive answer on God's plan for the world, John shared with me in private, "Wow, she is a real Christian!" I asked John if he agreed with the person's interpretation, and he said, "No, but she has the Bible on her side." Well, she had verses on her side, but I am not sure she had the Bible or God on her side. But that is my opinion. I think God takes special delight in a good argument!

As you can gather the questions about what to do with the Bible, *How do I read it?* and *What authority does it have?* are two of the most-asked questions that I have received. Here are some basics that I have come to believe are good starting points for reading the Bible with an open mind and inquisitive heart.

The Bible is a library of books composed, edited, and reedited by humans over a period of close to two thousand years. You might hear a pastor ending the reading of a Bible passage with the words, "Hear the word of God." I think it would be better to say, "Hear the words of ancient humans who were seeking to listen to what God might have been saying to them and might still be saying to you and to us." This is, in my opinion, more true to the historic reality but too long!

The Bible is a collection of varying genres (types of literature). The Bible contains creation myths, founding stories, poems and journal entries, theological musings, interpretive narratives, prophetic declarations, and hopes for the future.

The Bible is not consistent. The variety of genres have a variety of perspectives. The Bible is a collection of thoughts, beliefs, and doubts expressed through the ages. Theological ideas (e.g., sin, Satan, monarchy, justice, life after death) developed over time. For example, Satan appears in the book of Job as part of God's heavenly cabinet. Later, Satan morphs into the devil, the tempter, the fallen angel, who seeks to lead humans away from God. Satan resides in hell with his demons and the "wicked," those who are condemned to eternal punishment. But the author of the first psalm compares the wicked to dust that just blows away; they are no more (Ps 1:4). In Ps 139 (verses 7–8) there is nowhere to go that is outside of God's presence. Even in Sheol, the place of the dead, God is there too. Sheol in this psalm is not the *hell* of later development.

Yes, there are many verses that suggest an eternal damnation. To offer but one example, in Matt 13 Jesus explains the parable of the weeds (verses 36–43). As argued in the previous chapter, I don't think these are the words of Jesus. Rather, they are the interpretation of Matthew. Whatever the reality, a place of judgment is described as a "burning furnace," where people who sin will weep and grind their teeth for eternity. This description of hell as a fiery furnace has flamed the imagination of faithful Christians for centuries, used by those in power to control the masses.However, this interpretation hardly reflects God's mercy, forgiveness and love for all.

The books of the Bible reveal that indeed "history is written by the winners." The Hebrew Bible is the expression of ancient Israel. We don't know what the perspective of the "losers" (e.g., Amalekites and Canaanites) might have been. The enemies of Israel are all described as bad actors, and anything bad that happens to them was justified. When certain passages describe God directing the Hebrew army to completely and utterly destroy the enemy, I think this is more a projection of what the winners believed than it was a direct order from God. We know from history that this belief that God is on the side of whoever declares it, leading victors to do whatever they want to the defeated, leads down a very oppressive and violent path.

The monarchies of David and Solomon are described as the way God wanted it. However, there are other voices in the texts that suggest that the monarchy was not what God intended. Rather, a looser confederation of the tribes was truer to the divine intent. I don't think one should ever claim with complete certainty to know what God demands other than to love God and love your neighbor and to follow the golden rule.

Some would argue that you should follow the Ten Commandments. In a general way, I agree. But even the first biblical scholars, priests, scribes, and rabbis realized that there were many ways to interpret those commandments. The commandments state, "You shall not kill." But what does that mean during wartime? Is killing in self-defense, OK? Is killing of the enemy defensible? And how does one "honor one's mother and father?" Does that mean to do whatever they tell you no matter what? I hope you can see that it is not all that simple.

There are mood swings in the Bible—everything from thankfulness and absolute certainty to depression, lament, and cynical doubt. Read the psalms and you will get a full dose of every emotion. The prophets make declarations with lively passion against corrupt politicians and self-righteous religious folk.

In the letters of Paul in the New Testament, Paul gives advice and seeks to answer the questions raised by the members, for example in Corinth and Ephesus, to name but two of the early Christian communities. We know of (because Paul alludes to them) early Christians who didn't agree with Paul. Too often the reader defaults to the binary that Paul is always right, and therefore his opponents are always wrong. But we don't have the writings and opinions of those who disagreed, only Paul's reaction to them. Most likely those who disagreed with Paul and had another vision for the early church were faithful people with simply another opinion.

What Is the Bible and How Do You Read It?

Every Bible reader "picks and chooses." Liberals do it. Conservatives do it. Too often this criticism is thrown as a dart seeking to burst the alleged hypocritical balloon of the opponent. It is important that we realize that there are numerous and often conflicting passages that should keep us humble from any overconfidence that we have the "right" answer, yet we are drawn to those texts that confirm our opinions and shape our worldview. As has been a refrain throughout this book, start somewhere and then keep an open mind, be in a community of trust where thoughts, opinions, and interpretations can be shared without judgment. New truths and nuances, variations on the theme, will be revealed and keep you interested!

There may be other "how to read the Bible" basics, but I'll stop for now.

My advice for you is this: read the Bible with curiosity and a highlight marker. What catches your attention? What attracts you? What repels you? What sparks your imagination and curiosity? Let your questions guide you.

John Steinbeck, in his classic novel *East of Eden*, puts these words into the mouth of his character Samuel Hamilton, "Two stories have haunted us and followed us from our beginnings. We carry them with us like invisible tails—the story of original sin and the story of Cain and Abel. I don't understand either of them. I don't understand either of them at all, but I feel them."[1] When you read the Bible, try to feel rather than understand. Trust your gut. What resonates? What repulses? Read the stories of the Bible with fascination and awe, with some curiosity and imagination.

Is the Bible true? This question was raised by more than one person in the small group. Several of the participants had gotten into conversations with Christians who believed in the literal/factual truth of the Bible. The defense of this stance usually is stated in the question, "Well, if you don't believe that the seven-day creation story or the universal flood narrative of Noah and the ark are true and factual, then why believe that Jesus really rose from the dead or anything else?" Another usual defense is, "Would God

1. Steinbeck, *East of Eden*, 1.

lie?" These questions present all or nothing propositions that leave many seekers speechless. Being constrained to a binary choice—the Bible is either true or false—is very limiting.

The "truths" that the Bible points to are much more nuanced and better approached by storytelling, poetry, and metaphor. Science has proven that the universe was not created in seven days but rather expanded over billions of years. We know factually from fossil evidence that humans evolved and did not live during the time of dinosaurs. This is true. However, that doesn't mean that the authors of the biblical books were lying.

Robert Burns, the poet laureate of Scotland, is known for his famous line, "My love's like a red, red rose."[2] It can be true that love is beautiful. It can be true that love is prickly with thorns sometimes. Is only one answer correct, making the others false? In that opening line, Burns is asking a deeper question about the "truth" of his love.

Flannery O'Connor, an American author known for her short stories, wrote fictional tales revealing great truths about rural, small towns in Georgia in the fifties and sixties.[3] Her made-up tales and her characters reveal both a deep appreciation for and a searing critique of the Jim Crow South. While not factual, her stories are true. All good fiction points to profound truths. Likewise, artists, poets, musicians, philosophers, and theologians all engage the seer, hearer, and reader to expand their understanding of the world both in its intimacy and grandness—not with facts but with words that illumine the larger mystery. In this they join the scientist who wonders at the mystery and the larger questions and then follow their craft to answers which, according to the scientific method, can always be expanded upon and refined. In this way all truth points beyond itself.

Jesus told stories, parables, that were metaphors, calling the first readers/hearers to broaden their understanding of the "truth"

---

2. Burns, "Red, Red Rose," line 1.

3. See for instance the story "Revelation," in O'Connor, *Complete Stories*, 488–509.

What Is the Bible and How Do You Read It?

about the kingdom of God, forgiveness, death, redemption, grace, compassion, hospitality, and sacrifice.

The more important question than "Is this true or not?" is "What truth might it point to?" and "Are you going to shape your life by it?" Reading the creation story as literally true limits the truth of the story.

Jews and Christians revel in the mystery of a faith in a creative power that delights in creating, loves the creation and calls it good, and invites humans to care for it and each other. This is not true in a scientific sense, but shaping your worldview around these creative "truths" calls you into an engaged life of awe and wonder which leads to commitment and care. I think that the late Professor Marcus Borg provided a wonderful way of seeing all Scripture as "metaphorical," describing reality in an open-ended way that invites the reader to question and wonder.[4] Saint Paul couldn't have expressed it better when he wrote, "Now we see a reflection in a mirror; then we will see face-to-face. Now I know partially, but then I will know completely in the same way that I have been completely known" (1 Cor 13:12). What Paul writes is true.

We can never know with complete certainty. The truth is always larger and is "out there," as Agent Dana Scully, played by the actress Gillian Anderson, expressed in the hit 1990s television show *The X Files*. The active, seeking faith of one who follows Jesus will lead to truth upon truth, always pointing beyond itself.

Another question related to the Bible concerns how the Bible came to be and how the various books were chosen. There are many scholarly books that can lead you into the details of these fascinating questions.[5] I think it is enough to know that it took a long time for the Hebrew Scriptures to come together. Most probably, the formation of the Hebrew Bible occurred while the Israelites were in exile in Babylon 597–538 BCE, reflecting upon their ancient past. Some still contend that Moses himself wrote the first five books of the Bible, known as the Pentateuch. But that cannot be right. With some degree of confidence, scholars agree that

---

4. Borg, *Heart of Christianity*, 36.
5. See Barton, *How the Bible Came to Be*; Beal, *Rise and Fall*.

King David wrote some of the psalms, and there were prophets named Isaiah, Jeremiah, Micah, and Amos, for example. But even the psalms and the writings of the prophets reveal works shaped by many hands over centuries.

No one knows the identity of the authors of most of the books of the Hebrew Bible. Many, if not all, of the collected narratives show the signs of multiple sources and editors. The book of Daniel is from a much later time during the reign of Antiochus IV Epiphanes (175–163 BCE). The Hebrew Bible was pretty much fixed by the time of Jesus.

The New Testament had a shorter but similar process of composition. There are obvious signs of editing and rewriting of source material in all the books of the New Testament. The letters of Saint Paul (Galatians, 1 Thessalonians, 1 and 2 Corinthians, Romans, Philippians, and Philemon) were likely written between the late forties and early sixties of the common era. The Gospels (Matthew, Mark, Luke, and John) were written sometime between 60 CE (Mark) and 110 CE (John). Other letters written in the name of Paul and other disciples were added.

In 367 CE, Athanasius, bishop of Alexandria, published his Easter letter listing the books of the New Testament that we recognize today. Athanasius seems to be passing on what was pretty much already recognized throughout the Mediterranean region. However, there was a great deal of fluidity in the process. There were many stories about Jesus and Paul being written and shared throughout the region for many years. There were competing evangelists and church leaders, small communities that held to certain traditions and narratives.

Scholars have uncovered many early writings from various places—some that are more mystical in style, some perhaps written by women, some which describe Jesus in a different way than the Jesus we have come to know through the Gospels.[6] There have been scholarly arguments presented that some of these texts were considered dangerous and heretical in the sight of the increasingly

---

6. Elaine Pagels has researched the noncanonical Gospels throughout her career. See Pagels, *Beyond Belief*.

male-dominated leadership of the church and therefore suppressed. This is probably true. For those wanting to dig deeper, the study of first-century Christian texts is exciting and fascinating.

What is true of both the Hebrew Bible and the New Testament is that no one possesses the original text of any of the books of the Bible. Roman Catholic Bibles include several books, not in the Hebrew Bible or in the Bible used by Protestants, that were written in Greek not too long before the beginning of the Christian era.

The Bible that we have before us is the collection of writings that communities of faith recognize as authoritative—they tell the story that needs to be told. The Bible passes down ancient wisdom, thoughts, convictions, perspectives, and interpretations that identify communities both Jewish and Christian that continue to develop in the present and will do so into the future. Opening the Bible today is joining the centuries-old conversation of those who have circled the mysteries of life since our ancestors looked into the skies and into their own internal motivations and wondered *why?* The Bible is the living artifact that indicates that we have always longed to live and love the question.

CHAPTER 8

Is Christianity the Only Way to the Mountaintop?

"Bapu Gandhi said, 'All religions are true.' I just want to love God," I blurted out, and looked down, red in the face.

—YANN MARTEL, *LIFE OF PI*

DURING THE SECOND GATHERING of the small group someone asked, "Can we have confidence in Christianity when there are so many choices and differing interpretations? Is one more correct than the other?" What is the relationship of Christianity to other faith traditions?

Traditionally Christians are told to believe that Jesus is the best and final answer to all of life's questions. He fulfilled the historic yearnings of ancient Israel, who longed for a messiah to come. While many Christians are respectful of other religions, still it is presumed that no other tradition measures up. Furthermore, for those Christians who believe that the goal of religion is to get into heaven and to do so you must believe in Jesus, then no other religion than Christianity can get you to where you long to go. This mindset leads to fear and suspicion of other religions. There is, in some quarters, even fear that attending a yoga class might draw a Christian away from the faith because yoga comes from an Eastern religious tradition stressing mindfulness and balance.

But what if this is not the only way to think about Christianity's relationship to the multiple religions and faith traditions of the world? What if it doesn't come down to a "right and wrong" answer or "We have the ultimate truth and you don't"?

I love that confession in Yann Martel's novel *Life of Pi*.[1] Pressured to choose one religion over another, Pi expresses his frustration about having to make a final decision and his yearning to simply love God. And really, isn't that one of the fundamental aspects off all religious longing? Pi's confession speaks to me, and I believe that they express the feelings, frankly, of most people. We "just want to love God." While some affirm that only Christianity is the true, right, and final expression of God's will and purpose for the world and its people, many others believe that Christianity is one way among many of reaching for and responding to a sense of the divine, a higher power, a truth which is larger than self. Personally, I celebrate the different faith traditions and want to learn from them. It is not a zero-sum competition with one religion being right and all the other religions being wrong. This limited competitive understanding has led to violence and war, pitting culture against culture and religion against religion, and a belief that God is on one side and not the other. No wonder that my atheist friend believes that religion is the single most evil force in the history of the world. I don't agree with him, but I understand how he could come to that conclusion.

It is true that the practices and beliefs of the many religious traditions are varied, but the similarities far outweigh the differences. Beginning to immerse myself in the prayers, poems, and expressions of faith shared by many Native Americans, I am struck by their awareness of the divine, their awe at the natural created beauty, their hope for an afterlife, their call to treat every living

---

1. Martel, *Life of Pi*, 69.

thing with respect, and their practice of walking gently upon the earth.

It is from Judaism that we learn about God's delight in creation, the prophetic call for justice, and that God is a saving, active, forgiving, caring power. Yes, God gets angry with the people when they turn their back on what God desires for all of humanity, when they continuously turn away from loving God. Yet, even in God's frustration, God calls us to return, repent, repair, and restore. It is the Jewish faith that teaches *tikkun olam* ("repairing the world")—that humans are to care for the world, actively seeking to improve and preserve creation, acting as gentle stewards of the earth and ensuring justice for all beings.

Just as Christianity arose from Judaism, so too did Islam arise from its forebears having a similar but different take on the common ancestor of all three religions—Abraham. One doesn't need to be an expert to see the overlap and convergence of fundamental religious beliefs of those already mentioned and Buddhism, Hinduism, and the ancient religious traditions from the East.

Historical context, geographical location, and cultural norms all shape people's religious beliefs and practices. Sometimes I wonder what I would have become had I been born into a Jewish family. I suspect I would have become a rabbi.

I think the seeker, the one who loves and lives the questions, leans into the complexities, leads with curiosity, and should be open to the truths and wisdom of the varieties of the religious experience. Being a Christian is right for me. However, Judaism is good too, as is Islam and Hinduism and Buddhism and native religions of every culture. Thích Nhất Hạnh ("father of mindfulness"), the Vietnamese Buddhist monk, peace activist, prolific author, poet, and teacher, wrote a book called *Loving Buddha, Loving Christ*, celebrating the similarities of these two faith traditions and showing how Buddhists and Christians can appreciate and learn from each other.[2] The faith journeys of individuals are too diverse to limit them to one.

---

2. Nhất Hạnh, *Loving Buddha, Loving Christ*.

Jesus is the example that I seek to follow. I have learned and continue to learn from his life and teaching and from those Christians who have mentored me on how to be a more prayerful, compassionate, and loving person. If my life, shaped by the life and teachings of Jesus, draw others to follow Jesus too, well, that is a good thing. But life is too short and too complex to limit people's experience and, worst of all, to condemn their journeys.

My experiences have led me to believe that sooner or later one must "put a stake in the ground" and love God the best they can. At some point it is necessary to say, "These are my people" and "This is where I am dropping my suitcases." But I don't believe that Christianity is the only right place to call home.

Martin Luther, the German monk who started the Reformation in the sixteenth century, is believed to have declared, "This I believe, I can do no other." Those words resonate with me. However, my confession of my belief does not dismiss the confessions of others. On the contrary, all our confessions add to the richness of diversity that I think pleases God.

My advice is to start where you are. If you were raised a Christian, then really immerse yourself in it; don't be too quick to judge or change. Christianity has a deep and long tradition of contemplative spirituality, political activism, communal sharing, and inspiring worship. Thankfully, over the past few generations the diversity within Christendom has begun to be celebrated: intellectual Presbyterians copying the immersive contemplation of Celtic Christianity, the liturgy of Roman Catholicism, and the pacifism of the Anabaptist traditions. Foundational to Christianity in all its forms and expressions is a belief that love wins, humans are made in the likeness and image of God, and creation is good and should be cared for.

Of course, each religion has its emphasis and uniqueness. The uniqueness of Christianity centers around the person of Jesus as the embodiment of God. And part of that embodiment means that God suffers and allows Jesus (the "Son"—incarnation, flesh and blood) to suffer and die. Yet even unjust suffering can be redemptive, and death is not the end. According to the Christian tradition,

Jesus rises from the dead, sharing this resurrection power with us. These are deep and powerful concepts that for me and for many have been transformative—life changing. This is the lens through which I look at the world.

However, claiming Christianity doesn't mean I don't appreciate and can learn from the ancient wisdom of other faith traditions. Furthermore, it doesn't mean that I am right, and others are wrong. To do so seems limiting and counter to the open, curious spirit of a follower of Jesus. We learn so much from others.

In January 1985, music's biggest stars gathered to record "We Are the World," a song to raise money for those suffering famine and drought in Ethiopia and Sudan. Those who attended the recording included Michael Jackson, Tina Turner, Bruce Springsteen, Diana Ross, Stevie Wonder, and Bob Dylan, to name just a few of the musical superstars of that era. Bob Dylan, one of the most influential musicians in American history, wasn't comfortable singing his part. He couldn't get his timing right. He was timid in the company of all the other great musicians. Stevie Wonder took Bob Dylan aside. Impersonating Dylan's nasal voice, Wonder showed Dylan how to sing his part.[3] Stevie Wonder and Bob Dylan couldn't be more different in background and style. Yet here were two of the most iconic musicians alive, one learning from the other, imitating and teaching, sharing knowledge, appreciating the monumental gifts of each. To me this is an example of how we learn from, imitate, and teach one another, celebrating the gifts and truths of the variety of the religious experience. Bob Dylan didn't stop being Bob Dylan after that night; neither did Stevie Wonder stop being Stevie Wonder. But in their interaction Dylan was freed to sing his part, and the result was the recording of multiple voices for the good of all.

---

3. Nguyen, *Greatest Night in Pop*.

CHRISTIANITY AND JUDAISM

Christianity's historic relationship with Judaism has been fraught, to say the least. Christianity arose from Judaism, claims the Jewish Scripture as its own, and affirms Jewish beliefs taught in the Hebrew Bible, its demand for ethical behavior and communal care. Jesus was Jewish, and so were his first followers. He came out of the prophetic reforming tradition. To my understanding, Jesus didn't come to start a new religion. Rather, he seemed to be agitating his fellow Jews of first-century Palestine to reimagine what God was calling them to be and do. He was calling them to live the kingdom, reform the rules that no longer made sense, and be the children of God in a new way. Paul, the true founder and organizer of the church, who interpreted the practical and philosophical meaning of Jesus' resurrection to the Mediterranean world, was Jewish. If we are to believe the tradition, Paul was a trained Pharisee, part of a Jewish school that had a particular way of practicing the Judaism of the day. The Pharisees sought to contemporize traditional Judaism. From the Gospel accounts, you glean that the Pharisees had varying views of Jesus. Some were attracted, sensing similarities of thought. Others saw Jesus as a threat. Jesus affirmed the Pharisees' desire to learn and interpret anew the traditions and teachings. Yet, he was quick to call them and others out for their self-righteousness. Jesus and the Pharisees were siblings within the same Jewish family.

When it comes to Paul (also named Saul), I agree with those scholars who argue that Paul never thought that he left Judaism even as he preached the resurrection of Jesus to the early church. Paul came to believe that Jesus reinterpreted Judaism for a new age. Most Jews of the first century (and up to today as well) disagreed with him. Nevertheless, it wasn't until after the destruction of Jerusalem in 70 CE that Judaism and Christianity began to move along divergent paths.

To my mind, one of greatest tragedies of human history has been the divergence of Christianity—the offspring—from its parent religion, Judaism. Assigning blame for the separation is shrouded in history. However, once Christianity was adopted as the religion of imperial Rome, the split was final, and Judaism was cast as the "Christ killers" and enemies of Christianity.[4] Since then, and even into today, persecution, pogroms, violence, and anti-Semitic stereotypes stain and tear the fabric of our common life and shared faith identity.

Christians must confess to its complicity to this horrific historic fact and continue to seek for repair and restoration. To my mind, Christian usurpation of Judaism's Scripture, fundamental beliefs, and ethical norms, claiming that Jesus is the answer to Jewish longing and then blaming Jews for not accepting Jesus as the Messiah, is the historic and violent wedge that the church is guilty of driving in to divide the children of Abraham.

I believe that it is vitally important to address the traditional belief that Jesus particularly and Christianity generally fulfilled all of Jewish expectation and answered all the questions raised in the Hebrew Scriptures.

As you read the birth narratives in the Gospels of Matthew and Luke, you will notice the numerous citations from the Hebrew Scriptures that are said to be "fulfilled" in the birth of Jesus. For example, in Matthew we read, "Now all of this took place so that what the Lord had spoken through the prophet would be fulfilled: Look! A virgin will become pregnant and give birth to a son, and they will call him, Emmanuel. (Emmanuel means 'God with us')" (Matt 1:22–23).

What does it mean to fulfill something? The general definition of "fulfillment" means a coming to fruition of a prediction or a deliverance of an expectation. Traditionally, Christians have taken for granted that Jesus "fulfilled" the generational longing of the Jewish people for a messiah. It is a one-way and final completion of a hoped-for outcome. There is only one way to interpret the passages, and Christians have the right answer.

Yet I have come to understand the verb "fulfill" and its noun form, "fulfillment," as having more than one static, final meaning which implies a single, direct cause-and-effect culmination of an

---

4. Carroll, *Constantine's Sword*, 7–8.

expectation. Yes, the Hebrew Scriptures are full of longing and expectation. The Jews in exile want to return to Jerusalem. There is a yearning for someone from the "root of Jesse" (King David's father) to become king and restore the fortunes of Zion. The famous passage from Isaiah (7:14—written centuries before the birth of Jesus) that Matthew quotes to "prove" that Jesus is "Emmanuel" does not hold the same gravitas for Judaism. For Jewish commentators, the *alma* ("maiden") of virginal status who is pregnant with a child to be named Emmanuel is a contemporary of Isaiah. The prophecy is being fulfilled. The maiden and child are a sign that Israel will be home soon.

Another set of Jewish texts that have become crucial to Christian identity are the famous passages that describe a "suffering servant" (Isa 42:1–4, 49:1–6, 50:4–11, 52:13—53:12). Christians believe that Jesus fulfilled these expectations. Jesus was the Suffering Servant. Indeed, when you read the passages from Isaiah and then read the New Testament accounts of the crucifixion of Jesus, you can see the connections. And yet, when you talk to rabbis and Jewish biblical scholars, they would contend that the "Suffering Servant" is not one person who will appear in the distant future but rather a collective personification of the "children of Israel" who were, at the time of Isaiah, living in exile in Babylon.

Is this a question of right and wrong interpretations? I don't think so. Rather, we need to rethink what "fulfill" and "fulfillment" might mean. Take the word "fulfill" and separate the two words that combine to make the one word: "full" and "fill." Perhaps a better way of understanding what the word "fulfill" can mean is by switching the order of the two words. Now you have "fill-full." One passage can be filled full of meaning—different, rich, abundant, and multiple "true" meanings. Each generation can add to the fullness! For Christians, Jesus is the baby that reveals God's gracious intentions for the world, but not at the expense of what Jews believe. For Jews, the figure of the suffering servant has been filled full of meaning again and again through the centuries as Jews have been victims of horrific evil (exile, pogroms, persecution, and the Shoah), often at the hands of Christians. Yet, this historical reality does not take away the power of what Jesus represents and is for those who believe in him as the Christ.

For Christians, Jesus filled full the meaning of what the Messiah would be and do—even if Jesus didn't actually fit the first-century expectation of the Messiah as a king that would kick out the Romans and restore Israel. Christians reinterpreted the expectation so that Jesus' kingdom was "not of this world." Some Christians believe that Jesus' desire to form the beloved community of God's kingdom continues to be fulfilled every time a community seeks to express hospitality, forgiveness, nonviolence, and justice, living out the command of Matt 25 or of the Beatitudes of Matt 5. Other Christians believe that the fulfillment of their hopes and dreams of this kingdom will be in the afterlife or in the future.

For many Jews, the existence of Israel is the filling full of the hope and expectation of a restored community in the promised land. For many Palestinians, this filling full of the hope of the Jews is a disaster, a catastrophe (in Arabic, *nakba*), indeed the destruction of their hoped-for fulfillment for a homeland.

Some Christians read the entire Bible as a series of predictions that will come to fruition, being fulfilled in a specific way. They see in the formation of Israel the intermediate step of the fulfillment of the promise that Jesus will soon return on a one-way historical timeline. Hence, conservative Christians are some of the most pro-Israel Americans there are. However, in their narrow interpretation, Israel and Judaism ultimately will end up on the wrong side of history unless they accept Jesus as their Messiah. I believe that this is a dangerous misreading of the Scripture and frankly anti-Semitic.

I have always liked my friend the rabbi's answer to the question of when the messiah will come: "The messiah will come only when he is no longer needed." Meaning, I think, that the filling full of the hopes and aspirations of Jews and Christians and all people of good faith and good will is in part up to us in the here and now. We are to be the people that bring in the messianic age by living it the best we can, not waiting for a time that may never come.

Is Christianity the Only Way to the Mountaintop?

Christians and Jews share so much in common that there is much to celebrate and much to learn. I have always liked the words of the late Jewish theologian Franz Rosenzweig, who wrote, "I see Christianity as a sister religion to Judaism, as a form of 'Judaism for the Gentiles.'"[5] What a gracious way of addressing a relationship that has been defined mostly by the violence that Christianity has perpetrated on its ancestors. Christianity does not answer all the questions and longings of the Hebrew people found in the Hebrew Scriptures. Rather it continues the journey of loving and living the questions of faith, deriving new ways of looking at age-old problems, filling full the hopes and aspirations that we all share.

My attempt at an answer to the question of Christianity's relationship to other religions and particularly with Judaism is to lead with curiosity. If you are Christian-adjacent, first be open minded about the fullness of the Christian expression. Learn about Jesus; study the practices and varieties of the religious experiences of those who identify with Jesus. Borrow from other faith traditions what works for you. Honor and respect the faith expressions and practices of others. Celebrate the similarities. Be interested in the differences. Purity is not the goal when you are, like Pi, just seeking to love God.

Apparently, Mahatma Gandhi, the great disciple of nonviolence that illuminated the life, ministry, and activism of Dr. Martin Luther King Jr., insisted that he was a Christian and a Hindu and a Muslim and a Jew. Once again, Gandhi shows us the way to understanding and peace!

To me, one of the best examples of curiosity, sharing, and borrowing occurred in 1968 when the fourteenth Dalai Lama, the spiritual leader of Tibetan Buddhism, and Thomas Merton, an American Trappist monk, writer, theologian, mystic, poet, social activist, and scholar of comparative religion, met in India. There they had rich conversations about their respective faith traditions and how to respond to the war in Vietnam.

The Dalai Lama and Merton were dressed in the costumes of their religious communities. The Dalai Lama wore a thin belt

---

5. Kristol, "Christmas, Christians, and Jews."

around his waist, and Merton wore a thicker belt around his. Apparently while these two monumental spiritual leaders discussed issues of peace and prayer, the Dalai Lama noticed Merton's belt and in time adopted a thicker belt for his own robe. He later notes that he learned from Merton to "wear a thick belt instead of a thin chord around his waist."[6]

Harold Talbott, who brought these two great spiritual people together, noted in his memoir, "Imagine the Dalai Lama and Merton in deep conversation comparing Buddhist notions of compassion with Christian ideas of charity, the great religious leader all the time eyeing the monk's belt with some envy, and then later copying the monk's ways. Here we have an extraordinary example of religious learning—imitating the holy figure we admire—as well as living in the stereoscopic world in which one eye is on the cosmos and the other on a belt, a perfect reconciliation of time and eternity."[7]

I love this story of appreciation and imitation. This attitude of curiosity, attention, and gentle envy should be the guideposts to our appreciation and imitation of practices of other faiths. Yes, one eye on the cosmos and the other on the belt!

---

6. Dalai Lama, *Freedom in Exile*, 189.
7. Talbott, *Tendrel*, 127.

CHAPTER 9

Can Christians Be Political Without Being Right Wing?

The art of politics is to enable us to love.

—Arnold Toynbee, *A Study of History*

Just preach until the lonely feel loved, the homeless have homes, and the naked are clothed. Just preach until everyone everywhere knows that Jesus is love and God is alive.

Teresa L. Fry Brown

Can you be a Christian and get into politics? What does the Bible say about social action? Is God more of a Democrat or more of a Republican? How does one balance the more contemplative practices of prayer and gift discernment with the more active practices of protest and justice? Shouldn't politics and faith be separated?

While not being directly addressed, all the members of the small group that gathered in the fellowship hall shared that they were drawn to Forest Hill Church, in part, because of the congregation's active involvement in the local community and in social action.

The above questions are queries that I have been asked since I was ordained. I've been asking myself these questions since I was boy being dragged to civil rights marches by my parents in the late 1960s and writing my senior honors thesis on Dietrich Bonhoeffer, a German pastor and theologian who was hanged for being associated with the plot to assassinate Adolf Hitler a decade later. These questions challenge my identity as a Christian and agitate me to think deeply about my desire to follow Jesus.

For many inside and outside the church, these questions both attract and repel. While some are dissatisfied with churches that stress only personal salvation and personal purity, others are uncomfortable coming to church on Sunday feeling like they are coming to a political rally where there is little focus on prayer and contemplation. Russell Moore, one of the foremost spokespersons of evangelical Christianity who is critical of the rise of right-wing politics, expresses what many feel: "The church must stand against the way politics has become a religion and religion has become politics."[1]

In the late 1960's and early 1970's Forest Hill Church sought to end racial redlining and the practice of deeded communities that didn't welcome African Americans and Jews. It was one of the first congregations to ordain a woman to be an elder and to call a female pastor. It was in the lead in welcoming the LGBTQA+ community into full participation of leadership of the church. The Pride flag waves by the front door of the church. The church sponsors and supports a summer camp for transgender children and teens.

In 2016, members of the church formed an immigration task force in response to the Trump administration's draconian policies of border walls and separation of families. The church became a place of sanctuary for an undocumented woman who was to be deported. On the day of her deportation, with an ankle bracelet in place, she came to the church, where she lived for two years.

1. Moore, "President Trump."

Can Christians Be Political Without Being Right Wing?

Church members joined congregants from other churches and synagogues in holding prayer vigils in front of the regional ICE office.

This faithful political action has always been part of the spiritual DNA of the church. Busses were hired to take church members to Washington, DC, to protest the war invasion of Iraq after 9/11. The church became a leading member of the faith-based organizing collective "Greater Cleveland Congregations," a multifaith, interracial organization building power to change the policies of Northeast Ohio. The organization has both private and public relationships with senators, mayors, the governor, and city and county council members.

To me, it seems impossible that faithful living can be separated from political action. After two young Black men, members of the church, were accosted by police in their own mostly white community while selling raffle tickets for their high school football team, church members filled the chamber at the community's council meeting to protest this racial profiling. At the after-church meeting to debrief the experience, a Black member of the congregation shared that he didn't feel as if he fully belonged in the church. He challenged us to not only point the finger at institutions beyond the walls of the church but to look at ourselves as an institution which maintained racist and divisive norms. His comments drove the church into an ongoing introspective discernment about how Forest Hill Church could change and become a Beloved Community celebrating true racial equity.

Five church members organized a "Guns to Garden" gun buy-back program. The guns that were turned in were then disassembled, melted down, and turned into garden tools to manifest the call of Isaiah and Micah the prophets to transform the weapons of war and violence into tools for peace.

Although never endorsing a particular candidate, it is taken for granted both within the congregation and within the local community that the majority of church members are Democrats. The few Republican members stay pretty silent about their politics while remaining involved in the church. When asked, "Why do you stay?" they say, "Our friends are here," "I may disagree with the preacher but when my husband went to the hospital the pastors visited." One said, "Well, pastors come and go!" Their answers reveal that theological doctrine is less important than a sense of belonging. We will have more to say on this later.

Forest Hill Church is known as a very liberal and progressive faith community. As the pastor of this amazing congregation for thirty years, I always felt agitated by the question of how one truly is to welcome and accept the person with whom they disagree about things as fundamental as faith and politics. My desire was to create a safe space for disagreement while holding on to the deeper identity that we are all beloved children of God—sisters, brothers, and siblings of Jesus. This aspiration didn't always work when faced with hot-button issues of the day.

A pastor friend of mine preached a sermon the Sunday after the 2024 presidential election. Her focus was on comforting those who were disappointed in the results. She also laid out a call for faithful political action and engagement to push back against the anticipated policies of the new administration. She referred to the passages of Scripture found in Isa 58 ("Shout loudly; don't hold back; raise your voice like a trumpet"). The passage goes on to identify the homeless and the hungry as of particular concern for the faithful. She quoted a passage from Deut 10 welcoming the immigrant and stranger; she reminded people of Jesus' words in Matt 25:40: "When you have done it for one of the least of these brothers and sisters of mine, you have done it for me." In this passage Jesus names the hungry and thirsty, the stranger, the sick, and the imprisoned (verses 35–36). The passage is very clear: you are not a follower of Jesus if you are not serving the least and the lost. Most of the worshipers at this progressive engaged church were glad to hear this sermon. However, the pastor received an email expressing disappointment that she had "gotten political." Not too long before I retired, a member of the church let me know that he and his wife were leaving the church because my preaching was, likewise, "too political."

Usually what the discomfort means is not that the preaching is too political but that the message was perceived as too partisan and contrary to their more conservative political beliefs.

Yet, it is a fair critique. If I went to a church where the preacher gave a message that supports conservative policies about the immigrant, transgender persons, women's health concerns, and the election of Donald Trump, I would feel uncomfortable and would not return to that congregation.

Jesus' words found in Matt 22:21 and Mark 12:17 seem to suggest a way out. He is answering a question posed to him by a Pharisee about paying taxes to Caesar, the emperor. Jesus takes a coin and asks "whose image and inscription" are on the coin. The Pharisee answers, "Caesar's." Jesus responds, "Give to Caesar what belongs to Caesar and to God what belongs to God." Many interpret this verse to be saying that there is a clear separation between matters of faith and politics, church and state.

But is that really the case? Isn't Jesus asking the Pharisee to think more deeply about the issue, teaching that there is no separation of concern because everything belongs to God. The Pharisee's question implies that issues of faith and politics can be compartmentalized and separated. Jesus' answer suggests the opposite. The words and actions of Jesus, as described in an earlier chapter, lead not to Christian nationalism but to Christian compassion, generosity, and sacrifice for the common good, not for personal gain. The politics of Jesus is always critical of institutions and people that amass power at the expense of those in need.

Yet, herein lies a dilemma that we need to take seriously. For most, if not all, who attend church want to hear words of comfort and encouragement. They want to feel as if they belong to a community of care. They don't want to be riled up as much as calmed down. They want to do better at living their personal faith of prayer and forgiveness, of charity and care for the sick and the bereaved. Immediate, personal, and local concerns drive them into the pews to hear a message of acceptance and soothing forgiveness and grace. I get it and affirm it. Certainly, that is part of the mission of the church. Yet as the circle of concern is stretched beyond the immediate, local, and personal to include the ongoing, systemic, and global, tensions arise. Yes, churches should be a place of welcome for all. If congregations become a community only of those who vote the same way and are only focused on the political action of change, then something fundamental and formational is missing. Likewise, if a congregation stresses only personal salvation, purity, and charity at the expense of social justice and social action, then it too misses the mark.

It seems to me that the only way of holding both sides of this dilemma faithfully and staying in the tension is to name the tension. Jesus calls us to prayer, to spiritual discipline, and to form a community of acceptance and love. Jesus also calls us to civic engagement, pressing the powers that be to justice and equity for all.

The word "politics" in the United States is usually taken to mean the art of deal making and compromise between Republicans and Democrats. Politics has to do with power and who holds it. Being political is often defined as being untrustworthy. It often appears that politicians only seek after status and power, dismissing the real concerns of their constituents. But politics, rightly understood, is based on the Greek word *polis*, meaning "citadel," "city," or "community." So being political means to be involved in the place where you live. In the Hebrew Scriptures, Zion, the city of David, (Jerusalem), was founded to be the place where God was most present and the divine laws and commandments were faithfully lived. To Isaiah, Jeremiah, Amos, and Micah, the misuse of political and religious power was a sign of communal breakdown, the reason for God's anger and rejection of Israel and Judah, and the cause of the Babylonian exile.

The books of Judges and 1 Samuel are all about the struggle between two political parties: those promoting the looser, decentralized federation among the twelve tribes of Israel and those who wanted a centralized monarchy. Both parties claimed the blessing of God. Those pressing for the monarchy so that Israel could be like other kingdoms won the day, and Saul, David, and Solomon became the heroes and villains of legend.

The Jewish story is shaped by politics. Israel's history is an ongoing struggle to find their own political identity among the political powers of the age: Egypt, Assyria, Babylonia, Greece, and Rome.

The celebration of Hanukkah, which is now remembered by the lighting of candles and the giving of gifts, originated as a memorial to a political revolution as Judas Maccabeus and his followers drove out the forces of Antiochus Epiphanes IV. In 63 BCE, Pompey the Great and his Roman soldiers marched into Jerusalem, beginning Roman control of the politics of the region until the seventh century CE.

Jesus' birth is shaped by politics. Born up north in the Galilean town of Nazareth, Jesus grew up in a region known as a political hotbed of insurrection.[2] The birth narrative of Jesus, particularly in Luke's Gospel, is shaped by the politics of the day. Luke introduces the story of Jesus to Theophilus, generally agreed to be a Roman official of some standing. Many Lukan scholars have argued that the whole point of Luke's Gospel is to curry favor with Rome, showing that Christianity is not a threat, perhaps even seeking political protection for this new religion.[3]

As Luke begins to narrate the story, he informs the reader that all this takes place when Herod is king of Judah. In chapter 2, Luke again names the political leaders of the day: Caesar Augustus, the Roman emperor, and Quirinius, the governor of Syria. In chapter 3, the reader comes to know that now Tiberius is emperor, and Pontius Pilate rules over Judah, Herod oversees Galilee, Philip controls Ituraea and Trachonitis, and finally Lysanias rules over Abilene. Even the religious leaders Annas and Caiaphas are essentially political appointees under Roman control. In the final chapters of Luke's Gospel, Jesus is brought before Pilate and Herod before his crucifixion. The story of Jesus is shaped by politics.

Returning to the birth narrative, Luke sets Jesus to be the alternative to Caesar, and the kingdom of God that Jesus announces as the alternative to the empire of Rome. Jesus' miraculous birth

---

2. See Aslan, *Zealot*, 55.
3. Conzelmann, *Theology of St. Luke*; cf. Lentz, *Luke's Portrait of Paul*, 1–6.

recalls the miraculous birth of Augustus. According to Luke's narrative, when Mary, the mother of Jesus, meets her cousin Elizabeth, she is filled with the spirit and declares a political agenda that is revolutionary: scattering the arrogant, pulling the powerful from their thrones, lifting up the lowly, filling the hungry with good things, and sending the rich away empty (Luke 1:51–53).

Jesus' first sermon described in Luke 4:18–19 is nothing less than a radical agenda based on the words of Isaiah, where the poor have good news preached to them, the prisoners are released, the blind receive sight, and the oppressed are liberated. These are signs of the year of Jubilee, a hoped-for event every fifty years where debts are forgiven, slaves are freed, and land is returned to its original owners, signifying a time of social and economic reset within the community; essentially, it is a year of liberation and renewal.

This political/religious agenda contrasting the way of Jesus with the way of empire is again shown in the Beatitudes found in Luke 6 and Matt 5: "Blessed are" the poor, the hungry, and those who weep; contrasted with, "But how terrible for" the rich and the comfortable. These words were shocking then and equally shocking now to those of us who are Christians living in the richest and most comfortable nation in the world. No wonder the words found in the Gospels are not emphasized in many churches, or they are spiritualized as "the poor in spirit." The message is to be humble and patient, don't stir things up, and wait for the by and by or the afterlife. A misreading to be sure.

Jesus' message has an edge, dare I say a political edge, of changing the systems and structures of the world so that the petition in the Lord's Prayer is fulfilled: "Thy will be done on earth as it is in heaven." What Jesus seems to be saying is that the work of the beloved community is to model heaven on earth, to be the kingdom people in the here and now. The powers that be, both in the first century and in the twenty-first century, still tremble at this vision.

Furthermore, Jesus wasn't crucified because he encouraged people to "consider the lilies of the field." He was brought before Pilate and Herod because he was perceived to be a political revolutionary. Crucifixion was the Roman form of execution for rabble-rousers.

The politics of Jesus was shaped by nonviolence and a radical hospitality and inclusion. He challenged the empire and sought to reform the religious status quo. He caught the attention of both the political and religious leaders and was executed.

The politics of Jesus has not always been used as Jesus envisioned. Emperor Constantine used the faith to drive the expansion of his empire. The crusades brought ecclesiastical (church) and dynastic power to bear to retake Jerusalem from the Muslim forces. Christian political power was used to persecute Jews throughout the centuries, and Hitler manipulated the German church to support his anti-Semitic and hateful agenda.[4]

When Martin Luther broke from the Roman Catholic Church and started what is known as the "Protestant Reformation," it was as much of a political movement as a religious one. John Calvin wrote extensively about the proper faithful role of politics in seeking to create a more faithful city of Geneva.[5]

Pastors and devout Christians were on both sides of the Revolutionary War. In fact, it is believed King George III once called the American Revolution "that damned Presbyterian rebellion." The Reverend John Witherspoon, a Presbyterian pastor, signed the Declaration of Independence.

Before, during, and after the Civil War, preachers on one side used the Bible to support the enslavement of Black persons; and on the other, to press for abolition. Both sides claimed God on their side. President Lincoln freely used biblical references in his speeches.

In the twentieth century, Christians have been motivated by their faith to press for child labor laws and voting rights for women, as well as prohibition. In the last hundred years, those who sought to live a life of political activism and spiritual renewal, or those who caught a vision for an alternative way of forming

---

4. Carroll, *Constantine's Sword*, 10–12.
5. The subject of chapter 20 in Calvin's *Institutes of the Christian Religion*.

What's Faith Got to Do With It?

community, were killed for it: Gandhi, Dr. King, and Malcolm X, to name but three of the most famous religious leaders.

The civil rights movement began in church sanctuaries and basements. Sermons, prayers, and hymns inspired those who marched and sought change. Many faithful people were jailed or suffered bodily harm because of their desire to follow the way, the truth, and the life Jesus. John Lewis, Father Daniel Berrigan, Fanny Lou Hamer are three examples of faithful Christians who got into "good trouble." So, to say we should keep politics out of religion is to seek to remove a core and fundamental piece of the gospel.

The evangelical church, more known for emphasizing personal morality and salvation, became politically motivated on issues of equal rights, abortion, same-sex marriage, and gender identity. In the 1970s and 1980s, the Reverend Jerry Falwell Jr. called for the formerly nonpolitical Christians to rise up in a "Moral Majority" and use their political power to push back what was called a liberal, non-Christian agenda. In the last few years, the Reverend Dr. William Barber II is leading a new generation of faithful engagement in issues of civil rights and social equity.

This brief historical survey shows clearly that there has never been a separation of faith and politics since the beginning of Christianity. The question is how to interpret the politics of Jesus and follow it. There will always be disagreement, which suggests that there should always be room for questioning, self-reflection, and change. I think one can and should be guided by their deepest conviction but always have the humility to be challenged and to evolve. To my mind the key is to be faithful, which is shaped by curiosity and humility, and not ideology, which tends towards certainty and narrowness.[6]

Jesus continues to call us to a life of engagement, releasing the captive, and preaching Jubilee. Jesus' words are still the "marching orders" of those who seek to follow him. Those who are drawn to

---

6. David French is one example of an evangelical political commentator for the *New York Times* who I might disagree with theologically on some issues; however, I respect his faith and his political thinking, agreeing with him on the fundamentals of following Jesus.

this way, this truth, and this life will face certain agitation and, at times, opposition from those who are invested in the politics of selfish interest and the accumulation of dominating power. No doubt this side of the message of Jesus causes a great deal of discomfort to many because it demands not only personal but societal change. However, choosing to follow Jesus, being in community, seeking to celebrate the gifts, and sharing the abundance will help you get comfortable with feeling uncomfortable. The discomfort will indicate the way forward.

I use the word "agitation" a great deal. Think of the "agitation" cycle in your washing machine. In the action of stirring things up, the dirt is released, and you get clean clothes. Spiritual agitation works the same way. Shaking things up and turning things around, you come out refreshed and ready to continue the journey.

JOURNEY INWARD, JOURNEY OUTWARD

Throughout the years I have known many people who have committed themselves fully to a righteous cause, be it feeding the hungry, visiting the homeless on a cold winter's night, marching for the rights of marginalized people, getting out the vote, or organizing citizens to hold elected officials accountable. Often, however, these people, having given themselves to causes of equity, justice, fairness, and inclusion, burn out. Their energy depleted; they drop out and feel empty. Sometimes they find themselves overcommitted to something that doesn't bring them power and satisfaction. Committing to the politics of Jesus without cultivating the prayerfulness of Jesus will take it out of you.

During World War II, a young chaplain, Gordon Cosby, "became convinced of the futility of war and it was there that he saw how desperately people needed a deeper experience of faith than most churches are structured to offer. He promised God that if he survived the war he would dedicate himself to the pursuit of creating new structures and methods which he hoped would give the church greater integrity and help people enter the depths of discipleship and find the life that sustains."[7] From this vision he and his wife, Mary, founded the Church of the Saviour in Washington, DC. Its mission, simply described, is to help cultivate a deep well of spiritual energy, helping people find their "calling" (what they are most deeply concerned about and wanting to commit to).

Church members go through a long process of gift discernment, practice of prayer, and study of the Scripture in community until there is clarity about a direction for involvement. The phrase "journey inward, journey outward" expresses the process. The journey inward of prayer, discernment, and study leads the person on a journey outward of commitment and action. The journey outward leads the person to be refreshed for the work by returning to prayer and study in community. I think the contemporary church would be well served to follow the Church of the Saviour's model.

Not everyone is called to political action. But everyone is called to use their own particular gift for the service of others. Frederick Buechner, the Christian public intellectual, names the intersection of "your deep gladness and the world's deep hunger"[8] as the place where you will find a purposeful and meaningful life. However, being moved by the world's "deep hunger" will lead you into place of both spiritual and political growth.

Furthermore, there are seasons of action and seasons of contemplation. Certain stages of life affect the expression of your faith. Young parents with infants don't have the time and energy to lead the picket line; their focus is on the holy work of diaper changing. Older adults may not be able to join the march, but they can offer prayer, encouragement, and other forms of support.

At times saying "no," in order to detach and take care of yourself is the right thing to do. It is necessary and holy work. I remember the words of one very active parishioner who was going through a difficult time. She confessed, "I just need to sit in the pew and pray and sing hymns and listen to the choir and just be."

---

7. Church of the Saviour, "Origins"; see also Cosby, *By Grace Transformed*, 22.

8. Buechner, *Wishful Thinking*, 118.

A dynamic and welcoming community should celebrate the times and seasons of every life.

So, what is the relationship of faith and politics? It is very difficult, if not impossible, to separate. They are intertwined strands of one chord. Our faith is lived out in various communities: family, congregation, work, neighborhoods, cities, nations, and the international community. Seeking to walk the way, the truth, and the life of Jesus will lead you into interaction with others. Inevitably choices and commitments will have to be made. Sooner or later, one must stand up for what they believe. Guided by the teachings and life of Jesus, at some point you will find yourself in tension and perhaps even conflict. Speaking the truth in love to the powers that be, making those compromises that affect the common good, and working to bring a faithful equity to your community is political. However, what makes Christian politics different from the many political organizations is the journey inward of prayer, which we will cover in the next chapter.

CHAPTER 10

How Do I Pray?

But prayer, mature prayer is dominated by a sense of God. Prayer rescues us from a preoccupation with ourselves and pulls us into adoration and of pilgrimage to God.

—EUGENE PETERSON, *THE CONTEMPLATIVE PASTOR*

Be not forgetful of prayer. Every time you pray, if your prayer is sincere, there will be a new feeling and new meaning in it, which will give you great courage.

—FYODOR DOSTOEVSKY, *THE BROTHERS KARAMAZOV*

IN THE SMALL GROUP there were so many questions raised about the effectiveness of prayer. "I've tried praying and it just doesn't work." "I don't get what prayer is for." "I don't know how to pray." "What do I say, how do I do it?" Very few of the group participants prayed before dinners, said prayers before going to bed, or had any kind of prayer practice. However, all the parents confessed that they wanted their children to pray, to give thanks for parents and grandparents. Everyone at the table shared a common desire to find a moment from the rush of their days and set aside some quiet time. "But how do you pray when you have to chase your kids around all day?" "I am so busy at work that when I come home, I just flop."

These concerns are not new. "I prayed that my son would be healed, but God didn't answer. My son died. I have lost my faith in a God." What do you say to a heartbroken mother? My brother Peter died of cancer when he was thirty-two and I was twenty-nine. I prayed daily for his healing. It didn't "work." Peter died. My own experience and the experience of the mother whose son died has been shared by countless others. Tragedies stretch one's understanding of prayer and its effectiveness. Everyone has grown tired of hearing the common response after yet another tragic mass shooting: "You are in our thoughts and prayers." Ann Weems has written a "prayer" that she can't pray for peace anymore, for mere words and desires don't change anything.[1]

Many times, people have relied on the words of Jesus found in John 14:13–14: "I will do whatever you ask for in my name, so that the Father can be glorified in the Son. When you ask me for anything in my name, I will do it." Heartfelt prayers are raised, but they are not fulfilled in hoped-for ways. Some lose their faith; others think that their faith isn't strong enough. If it were, then their prayer might have been answered. I think that a misunderstanding of what prayer is and means often leads to self-recrimination and doubt. I have come to experience prayer as more than bringing a wish list to God.

Several years ago, the country star Garth Brooks wrote a song titled "Unanswered Prayers."[2] He sings about the memory of his high school girlfriend. He prayed that God would bring them together in marriage. But many years later he stands with a different woman who is now his wife. They bump into the old high school flame, and it causes Brooks to reflect: "Sometimes I thank God for unanswered prayers." Brooks lyrics reflect the thoughts of another icon of popular music, Mic Jagger. In his famous song "You Can't Always Get What You Want," Jagger reminds us that while you

1. Weems, "I No Longer Pray for Peace."
2. Brooks, "Unanswered Prayers."

may not get what you want, sometimes you will get what you need. Jagger's insight is profound and helpful.[3] The answer to prayers may not be met immediately or in the hoped-for way. However, in time and with reflection you begin to detect that maybe what you were praying for then has been "answered," or a way has been revealed that broadened expectation and provided a new insight.

There is no pat answer for the grieving mother who lost her son. It is always better to remain silent and just be present. The best we can do is to support her in this life-changing journey. Perhaps in time she will find peace. Perhaps our actions are a better prayer than words and thoughts.

I have heard questions about prayer for as long as I can remember. This chapter won't provide a good and final answer to the mystery of prayer. My hope is to encourage you to create space and time to be still and open. I can't promise that prayer will provide answers. For me, prayer is not a "cause and effect" process. I don't know if I have ever received a direct answer to my prayer. Although I will say that I have experienced times when I have prayed to be open and hold things loosely and pay better attention and not try to expect anything, and something has happened that made me feel as if insight had been given.

I visited the hospital room of a man facing death. I was scared because I didn't know what to say. Before I walked in the door, I prayed, "Lord help me to get out of my own way. Remind me that you are already present in the room; I am not bringing you anywhere." That man and I had a profound conversation about death and dying. Answered prayer? I'll claim it. It may well have been that saying those words in what I believed to be the presence of God enabled me to be present too.

I do know of individuals who have had their prayers answered. I have known people who seem to have a particular gift for intercessory prayer—prayer for others. Some people have been given the title of "Prayer Warrior." I have encountered many a person who are grateful to be prayed for. The connection makes them

---

3. Jagger and Richards, "You Can't Always Get."

feel less alone. Knowing that people are praying for me have given me courage to face things and makes me want to give my best.

For me, prayer is a discipline of making space and time for naming that which is on my heart and expanding my limited horizons, connecting me with other people and places and with my higher power who I call God or Jesus.

People have asked me, "Do you pray to God or to Jesus or to the Spirit?" To me there is no difference. I pray my words to God. That is my tradition. Jesus prayed to God. I often end my prayers with "In Jesus' name." Again, it is the tradition I grew up in. There is no formula.

Christian prayer is relational. It is directed to a divine other that cares who we are and what we are praying about. Other traditions focus their prayers to other spirits, deities, or objects, or to nothing in general. Non religious individuals share with the "religious" meditative practices that are inner directed, helping them get in touch with things and feelings stirring within. I think it is all good.

There is a tradition within Christianity called "Centering Prayer."[4] In Centering Prayer one sits in silence, accepting whatever is revealed or not revealed, aware of distractions and gently laying them aside. One seeks to silence all voices but the voice of God. Some use a word like "Jesus" or "hope" or "love" to guide them back into the silence. Others softly chant a refrain. One that I love is the refrain from Marty Haugen's "Shepherd Me, O God."

Most days I pray as I take a walk. There is something about being in nature that opens me up. I give thanks for the day saying, "This is the day that the Lord has made. Let me rejoice and be glad in it!" I ask to be open to whatever happens. I lay out my schedule for the day and ask God to bless and keep me from being too controlled by it. I name my wife, Deanne, and my children, Jack, Meg, and Sarah, and my sons-in-law, Grant, and Jordan. I give thanks for them and give them a blessing. I bring to mind names of people who are sick or in the hospital or facing death. I picture in my mind and then focus on those who are going through tough times.

4. Keating, *Open Mind*.

I pray for places in the world where there is war, displacement, hunger, and oppression. For me, prayer connects me with others who I know and don't know; it increases my awareness. I want to live my daily life connected to others and aware of what is going on in the world. I confess those places of unrest and disconnect in my own being. I feel a need to name the discontent as a way loosening its grip on my life.

There are times when I am befuddled and feeling like a fake. I don't think I have enough energy for facing what I have to face in the day. I remind myself that I am a "beloved child of God" often, particularly when I don't feel that way. It is a kind of spiritual pep talk!

I repeat the words, "Lord have mercy on me, a sinner." I use these words not to make myself feel bad or produce shame. For me, these words remind me that I have broken places within. I have not lived up to my best. I have hurt others by my words and actions. Repeating the words "Lord have mercy" reminds me that I believe in forgiveness and that I am not judged by the worst things that I have ever done or continue to do.

I also use the words of the ancient prayer of Jesus known as the Lord's Prayer. I will say more about this prayer later because I think it provides a model for us all. I do pray for things. I pray for traveling mercies and safety when someone I know is on the road or in the air. I pray for healing. I pray for these things because they are important to me. I want safety for those I love. Whatever is heartfelt from a full heart, whatever you need to say, say it. But I have come to release control of the outcome. The poet Alice Walker reminds us not to expect anything, living "frugally / On surprise."[5]

In my prayers, I attempt to stay loose and open, attentive, waiting for the surprise—or not. I have to let go of that expectation too. In those moments when I have experienced an answer of sorts, usually my response is, "Wow!" and certainly, "Thank you!"

Those who are more skeptical about prayer often point to athletes thanking God or crossing themselves before a penalty kick or field goal attempt. I do not pray for my favorite sports team to win the championship. I share the discomfort when some athletes

---

5. Walker, "Expect Nothing," in *Anything We Love*, 90–91.

make the sign of the cross. I remember the words of Yogi Berra who allegedly said, upon seeing a batter cross himself before a pitch, "Sometimes I think we should just let God watch the game!" When players answer the first question after a big win with "I just want to thank God," I cringe. Yet even these displays are expressions of those who are aware of a larger moment in which they want to be present and ready and thankful for whatever. I appreciate that, even if it is not my way.

I share my prayer routine not because it "works" better than other forms and disciplines or because I think that everyone else should do as I do. Certainly not. But as you are pondering and living the question of what prayer is, how to do it, and whether prayer even matters, I want to invite you to think about what you are doing right now that gives you a sense of interior space, how you express the deepest yearnings of your heart, how you say thank you, and how you convey thanksgiving and joy, sadness and concern.

In Greek, the word for prayer means "to wish for"; in German, "to beg." In English, prayer implies a sense of entreaty or supplication. But in Hebrew, the word for pray is a reflexive verb meaning to "judge oneself." All four languages point to an aspect of prayer that is nuanced. Prayer is both a turning inward to take inventory of personal need and a turning outward to the concerns of others and the world.

I think Rachel Naomi Remen, in her collection of stories *Kitchen Table Wisdom*, says it well:

> I think that prayer may be less about asking for things we are attached to than it is about relinquishing our attachments in some way.... When we pray, we don't change the world, we change ourselves. We change our consciousness. We move from an individual, isolated, making-things-happen kind of consciousness to a connection on the deepest level with the largest possible reality.... Prayer is a movement from mastery to mystery.[6]

It takes practice to pray. Prayer is a discipline, like working out in a gym or playing scales and études over and over and over

---

6. Remen, "Pray Without Ceasing," in *Kitchen Table Wisdom*, 270–71.

What's Faith Got to Do With It?

again. Just as you cannot sit down and play a nocturne of Chopin without years of practice, or hit a golf ball two hundred and fifty yards straight down the fairway without hours at the tee, I don't think you will reach the depths of the power of prayer without doing it. However, playing chopsticks can be beautiful too, in its simplicity. Anne Lamott is on to something when she says the best prayer is "Help, Thanks, Wow!"[7] Just express what is on your heart and mind, and let it go from there. Stay open and observant to how you change, and pay attention to how your prayers change as you practice. Certainly note when you think your prayers have been answered.

Some feel very self-conscious praying both in public as well as in private. That is OK. I often feel that way too, and I am asked to pray a lot since I am a "professional"! When I am at a family gathering praying over a meal, I usually just let the words come, focusing on my thankfulness for the food and those who are gathered at the table. I often give thanks for those who made the meal and for those who raised and gathered the animal or grain that we are eating. I try always to remember those who are on the margins, who may not have enough food. However, there are traditional prayers—yes, even, "Good food, good meat, good God, let's eat!"—that at least cause us to pause before we dig in. To pause is important, to appreciate the food and the surroundings, to give a moment of awareness.

When I was a pastor preparing for the Sunday service, I would spend a lot of time writing my "prayers of the people." I wanted the words to flow and even tried to be poetic at times. In some denominations, the weekly prayers of the people are written in a prayer book. Some push back against these prepared prayers: "Only spontaneous from-the-heart prayers count." Certainly, spontaneous prayers can be powerful and poetic. But this is not always the case. Sometimes the prayer can be longer than a sermon! I had a good friend who once said about a pastor's spontaneous prayer, "He prayed just long enough for the biscuits to get cold!"

---

7. Lamott, *Help, Thanks, Wow*.

How Do I Pray?

Many beautiful prayers that speak to our deepest needs have been written through the ages. Just because they are not your words doesn't mean that they don't express the longings of your heart. Using a collection of prayers can be a wonderful encouragement.

I shared above that the prayer of Jesus, known to us as the Lord's Prayer, is very meaningful to me. I would guess that I recite the Lord's Prayer at least a dozen times a day. The words go down deep in my soul. I love that the prayer is ancient, as close to the real words of Jesus as we get. The prayer is about an intimate relationship with God, who Jesus calls "Father." Some would say that Aramaic word is better translated "Daddy." In my opinion, you can use "Mother" or "Parent" too—don't let nomenclature get in your way.

Jesus tells his ancient and modern disciples that our life in community with others should reflect how heaven works. To me, this is not about heaven being a faraway, separate place coming in the by and by but rather an invitation to live heaven now. I find it compelling that Jesus indicates how we are to live this kingdom life now: Get enough and share enough bread so that everyone eats each day. Forgive others, be forgiven, and let those past distractions go. Do what you need to do to restore relationships and repair the divisions. We are to stay away from evil. That is heavy; what some find evil, others find not so much. The word "evil" is dropped a lot in contemporary culture. However you define "evil," stay away from it and focus on the good, the true, the beautiful—follow your highest aspirations—don't get so caught up in doubt and self-concern that you miss opportunities. Don't give in to simple answers and selfish concerns. Sweep clean that which holds you back from stepping into the next ray of light that is before you.

I encourage you to paraphrase the Lord's Prayer for yourself. Not that it is final and better than the original, but see how it speaks to you today. Is there a word of the prayer, a sentence, that catches your attention?

The Lord's Prayer is a prayer that I will continue to pray daily during these days of disruption when immigrants are demonized, our natural wilderness despoiled, and the oligarchs gather for self-aggrandizement. We are called to stay open, be compassionate, gracious, and forgiving, to share our bread, to welcome the stranger, to walk lightly on the earth, and to turn from evil.

At Ghost Ranch, the Lord's Prayer was paraphrased by John Phillip Newell. I used it almost every morning when leading morning prayer at that magnificent spot in Northern New Mexico. Newell's words make the prayer come alive for me. Perhaps it will help you pray this prayer and make it your own.

> Ground of all being, Mother of life, Father of the universe
> Your name is sacred, beyond speaking.
> May we know your presence.
> May our longings be your longings
> In heart and in action.
> May there be food for the human family today
> And for the whole earth community.
> Forgive us the falseness of what we have done
> As we forgive those who are untrue to us.
> Do not forsake us in our time of conflict
> But lead us to new beginnings.
> For the light of life, the vitality of life, and the glory of life
> Are yours now and forever. Amen.[8]

The best advice I offer is to pray how you can, not how you can't! Sometimes groans and curses are prayers—the movement of energy away from yourself into space, a release of tension, of hopes, of fears, of dreams and disappointments.

Set aside time to be still. Put the soles of your feet on the ground. Breathe deeply. Roll your shoulders and loosen up. Clench your hands into fists and then release the tension. Call to mind those you love. Remember those who are in need. Connect your spirit to the spirit of longing in the world. Say thank you. See what words arise within you.

If you cannot find space and time, or don't have space and time for stillness, pay attention to yourself and what is going on inside as you take a walk, knead bread, change a diaper, fix dinner, or work out. Honor yourself and your thoughts and feelings, and see what comes of it.

---

8. From Newell's prayer book for use at Ghost Ranch. Used with permission from the author. See also Douglas-Klotz, *Prayers of the Cosmos*.

CHAPTER 11

What About Sex and the Bro Culture?

Sex is part of nature. I go along with nature.
—Marilyn Monroe

A relationship is not just about sex—it is much more than that. Sex is only a tool in love, not love itself.
—Abhijit Naskar, *Wise Mating*

Oh, your loving is sweeter than wine!
Your fragrance is sweet; your very name is perfume.
—Song of Solomon 1:2–3

"Why does the church care so much about sex?" "Why are priests celibate?" "Why do some churches still exclude gay people and women from being ordained?" "Does the Bible teach that there are only two sexes, and genders?" "Why do churches care about premarital sex?" Questions about abortion, pornography, divorce, living together, the role of women, clerical sexual abuse, and the so-called "bro culture" kept flowing. For those who seek to live the questions, there are a lot of questions to live when it comes to issues related to sex and sexuality!

I will not seek to answer comprehensively any of the questions raised. Honestly, I continue to have questions as my perspective has stretched through relationships and by experiences. The issues related to sex and sexuality are so personal and so complicated.

Yes, there are many Christians, shaped by a more narrow reading of the Scripture, who fear that God will harshly judge nontraditional beliefs or according to so-called "biblical norms"—assumed biblical norms that seek to limit sexuality, sexual expression, and identity to a binary choice and restricted hierarchical roles.

However, I think that for those who seek to follow the way, the truth, and the life of Jesus, there are guideposts along the way. Leading with curiosity, being honest with oneself and with others, trusting one's own experiences, and being true to shared biblical values of respect, hospitality, love, and openness will frame our responses to the myriad of confusing issues.

Everyone in the group shared the perception that the historic, traditional church's views of the related issues concerning sex were "regressive, oppressive, judgmental, and hypocritical." There was a shared common perception that Christianity was against the liberating cultural forces that—despite contemporary backlash—were moving forward in progressive and inclusive fashion. These young adults didn't want to be part of any church that harshly judged their friends, colleagues, and family members who identified as part of the LGBTQA+ community. While women were more vocal, men and women alike wanted nothing to do with the oppression or suppression of women and women's choices about birth and abortion, marriage, spousal relationship, family size, and child rearing. They were suspicious of what they described as old men and politicians meddling in their bedrooms and their choices of partners. What they wanted was support for their parenting through childcare, protection of their children, the acceptance of their identities, and help particularly for boys and young men. They didn't want their religious seeking shaped by fear, guilt, and obligation.

While not descriptive of every Christian or all churches and religions, the concerns and questions expressed by the group raised a fair and devastating critique of the institutional church and historic Christianity, and a reality that is hard to argue against.

In the Catholic Church, the Southern Baptist denomination, and within many conservative nondenominational churches, women are still not allowed to be priests and pastors. In some churches, a divorced person is not allowed to be a leader of the congregation. There are some Christians who still believe that premarital sex is sin and that unwed couples should live apart until they are married.

Sexual assault, abuse, and misconduct is still common throughout denominations, parishes, and congregations with pastors and priests using their personal and positional authority to rape young parishioners and peddle child porn. Usually, priests and pastors are enabled and abetted by spouses, colleagues, supervisors, and staff.[1]

It is true that most denominations now have policies and processes for the protection of the vulnerable and accountability of the perpetrator. While necessary and welcomed, the responses are long overdue and, in some cases, inadequate.

It is also true that there is less open hostility and suspicion for revealing oneself as non-cisgender or non-heteronormative than there was fifty years ago. Many Christian churches are now "open and affirming" or "More Light" churches, and the Metropolitan Church is a predominantly gay denomination. There are now pastors and lay leaders in churches that reflect the full rainbow identity of the LGBTQA+ community. While not going so far as to affirm nonbinary identities and relationships, even the Church of Jesus Christ of Latter-day Saints and the Roman Catholic Church have made moves to at least recognize the openness of the larger society.[2]

1. See Guiora, *Armies of Enablers*.
2. Rauch, *Cross Purposes*, 156.

What's Faith Got to Do With It?

However, the Westboro Baptist Church of Topeka, Kansas, still proclaims that "God hates fags." And while most conservative churches seek to be more "loving" ("love the sinner, hate the sin"), the message of judgment, shame, and sinfulness have driven countless members of the LGBTQA+ community away from the church and away from faith. So called "conversion therapy" is still proscribed in some congregations. Conservative Christians are at the forefront of removing books celebrating same-sex parents and fluid sexual identities of young people, and banning drag queen story hours. Furthermore, the Supreme Court has consistently supported conservative Christians' "rights" not to serve gay customers. There is a growing backlash against the LGBTQA+ community in the contemporary culture, which is empowering a backlash within conservative Christian churches. The tide of anti-queer prejudice which seemed to be receding in the past twenty years or so has come back in reactive fury.

Conservative Christian leaders and influencers shape pronouncements from the president and the director of health and human services, declaring that there are only two genders: male and female. Trans children are barred from sports and medical care.

Conservative Christians are at the forefront of the pro-life movement, cheering the end of Roe v. Wade. There are even a few on the Christian right who would question a woman's right to vote. Other conservative Christians would ban women from serving in the military. There are still churches that will not allow women to teach a Bible study to men.

This reaction to the more liberal direction of the culture in the past fifty years or so has even spawned a rising "bro culture," which generally seeks to reclaim the superior status of men and masculine traits, which are hard to describe in detail or in full but generally include aggressive male authority, muscular sexuality, anti-gay and anti-transgender opinion, and support for MMA (mixed martial arts, and similar pugilistic events). In part this "bro culture" and its "toxic masculinity" is a reaction to a larger and shared concern about the development of boys, teens, and young adult males. Recently, Aaron Renn, in his book *Life in the Negative*

World: Confronting Challenges in an Anti-Christian Culture, supports the influencers of the "manosphere" who seek to restore traditional masculinity as an antidote to the "new secular orthodoxies around sex, gender, and race."[3]

However, there is pushback to the pushback. In their recent podcast, *Saved by the City*, Christian podcasters Katelyn Beaty and Roxy Stone described how evangelical religion, grounded in traditional patriarchy mixed with male entitlement, create toxic working conditions for women, particularly in evangelical (Christian) churches, businesses, and non-profits.[4] Beaty and Stone describe how women in evangelical settings are maltreated and marginalized.

This right-wing retrenchment of traditional biblical morality is making its mark. The Pew study indicated that the one demographic that was growing in church attendance, claiming Christian identity, was the young conservatives.[5]

Sex, and particularly the issues around identity and gender, is probably still the single largest issue that divides Christendom. It is the third rail of religion. Denominations have spent many years fighting long protracted battles about what the Bible teaches or doesn't. Mainline churches have split over the issue of being open and affirming to the LGBTQA+ community.

The division in the church is certainly shaped by the forces of cultural change in the last sixty or so years. Since the 1960s, the issues of sexual ethics and identity have become central to our cultural conversation. This fact causes many who came to adulthood before then to either shake their head in confusion, accept the reality of the sea change, feel liberated by new expressions and identities, or remain entrenched in the cultural norms of pre-1960s America. Those born after 1970 generally are more open. Certainly, people born after 2000 feel like one's sexual identity and practice is almost a nonissue. Almost everyone, liberal and conservative alike, have gay siblings and friends or know people who are

3. Graham, "He Gave a Name." See also Renn, *Life in the Negative World*.
4. Stone and Beaty, "Evangelical Bro Code."
5. Smith et al., "Religious Landscape Study."

transitioning, who live together, or who have had sex long before even thinking about marriage. This has changed the conversation.

The more conservative, traditional, and older Christian would argue that their own teaching about sex is biblically based. They believe that the Bible teaches that sex is good not only for procreation but also for fun and expression of love. However, sex is to be saved for marriage and only for the expression of love between a man and a woman. Furthermore, for these Christians the Bible affirm only two genders. There are "natural" roles described in the Bible for men and women. To these conservative Christians, this perceived role confusion is leading to a breakdown in marriage, masculinity, and culture. There is little room for nuance or diverse expression. This kind of clarity is appealing to some.

However, to many others it is not clarity at all. It is not descriptive of reality, science, and common sense. It is driven by a narrow reading of the Bible and does not reflect the life and teachings of Jesus. As with all social and cultural change, there is both good and bad and lots of nuance, confusion, and questioning.

MY STORY

When I went to college back in the 1970s, I think I knew one gay person. Of course, there were many more, but I just wasn't aware. It wasn't until I went to divinity school that my eyes and mind were opened. My divinity school roommate, Bob, was gay. He and I shared many a deep conversation about how he came to know he was gay and what that was like for him. He listened to and tried to answer all my questions.

One evening while at dinner, Bob sat with me in the refectory and essentially "outed" a third of the student body. He taught me to be more aware of the unintentional signs I was giving off. I had no idea that there were so many brilliant and deeply faithful gay people. It is now embarrassing for me to admit this, but it was true.

As I developed friendships, I heard heartbreaking tales about parents who refused to accept their child's identity. I listened to new interpretations of biblical passages and began to understand that "biblical teaching" was not just lining up a few verses that seemed to point to only one answer.

My expanded awareness came during the HIV/AIDS crisis. I knew so many gay men who lived daily in fear that they would contract this horrific disease. That so many of my friends were deeply faithful people, drawn to ministry and to the church, affected my beliefs about God's acceptance, compassion, and celebration of the diversity of expression and life. Again and again, I listened to those who for years had lived in guilt and fear, heard words of judgment and hate, were called hurtful names, and were told they were anathema to God.

Many in the church relied, and continue to rely, on a few scattered verses of Scripture to confidently proclaim God's judgment against all gay people. But the seven verses usually noted (Gen 9:20, 27; 19:1–11; Lev 18:22, 20:13; Rom 1:26–27; 1 Cor 6:9–10; and 1 Tim 1:10) are hardly definitive. These references describe scenes of rape, male prostitution, pedophilia, and abuse. They have nothing to do with free, adult, tender loving expressions of sexual affection. There are no explicit biblical references to sexual relationships between women. Furthermore, there are no references to same-sex marriage, committed same-sex relationships, or bisexual or transgender persons.

While you will not find definitive biblical teaching on the multiple and complex issues of sexual identity, you will find multiple passages that welcome those who were considered "unclean" by the religious leaders of the day to the table of Jesus and that welcome the marginalized into the kingdom. Galatians 3:26–28 is a definitive text for me: "You are all God's children through faith in Christ Jesus. All of you . . . were baptized into Christ. . . . There is neither Jew nor Greek; there is neither slave nor free, not is there male and female, for you are all one in Christ Jesus." This text breaks down the binary divisions of the first century, and to me, it continues to describe God's intention for all human divisions to cease in the twenty-first century.

This passage from Galatians became a touchstone for me when I was a young associate pastor. I went to visit a gay man dying of HIV/AIDS. The church where he was raised rejected him; the pastor refused to visit. I was asked if I would go visit him.

George was lying on the couch of his apartment. He told me the story of his "coming out." He was secure in his identity and that God loved him as he was. He told me of the dreams he had been having of his gay friends and the love of his life who were all together and cheering him on from heaven, reaching out to him as he said to "drag him" home. I've never forgotten that visit and that conversation.

Honestly, even if more traditional Christians had definitive biblical references on their side, I would side with this man, this beloved child of God, secure in who he was, grounded in his faith, and looking forward to the adventure of what was to come.

In these past forty years, I have continued to grow in my awareness and support of the full LGBTQA+ community. I still have much to learn. But of this I am sure: God's love and acceptance of all the beloved children will ultimately trump exclusion and hate. That is easy for me to say as a straight white man. But it is important to say it nevertheless. I hope my actions confirm my words.

I am reminded of the words written by Archbishop Desmond Tutu, who knew a thing or two about overcoming the hatred and division of apartheid. His words resonate with me and speak to the enduring hope: "Goodness is stronger than evil; love is stronger than hate; light is stronger than darkness; life is stronger than death. Victory is ours, victory is ours through God who loves us."[6]

In these past ten years or so, I have heard the stories of individuals and families transitioning, seeking to find comfort in their identities, pushing through the hatred and misunderstanding of the larger culture. Most of these beloved individuals have been hurt and excluded from the church and the culture dominated by traditional Christian norms. What surprises me and gives me hope is that so many of these individuals still come knocking on the doors of the church, seeking to belong to a community of love that will accept them as full human beings made in the likeness and

---

6. Tutu, "Victory Is Ours," 80.

image of the creator. I believe that Jesus would throw the doors open wide! What saddens me is that so many have been hurt by the misuse of the words of Jesus, that the church has lost talented, faithful, beautiful people.

So, I believe that one who seeks to follow the way, the truth, and the life of Jesus must welcome everybody, especially those who any contemporary culture marginalizes or "otherizes." Trying to remain entrenched in the past only loses the future.

Coming to know who you are, what path to follow, what gifts you possess, and how to live your life is fraught for everyone. With compassion and hospitality, those who live the questions must lead with curiosity and love.

Forty years ago, when Deanne (my wife) and I met and fell in love, I think I knew of one friend who lived with his girlfriend. Of course there were many who chose to do this. We just didn't know them. Even after our engagement, we lived apart and tried to keep our sexual energy in check. It was just what Christian kids raised in the church were expected to do.

Thinking about it now, I don't feel embarrassed. It was right for us at the time. We agreed that this is what we wanted to do. Full disclosure: we were engaged in March and married in September of the same year! However, our choice in retrospect is rather quaint. Yes, there are still those who wear chastity rings and wait to have sex until marriage. Good for them. If that is their choice, so be it. Yet, in my forty years of performing weddings, I can remember one couple that chose not to live together before the wedding ceremony. They got divorced. I have not kept track of all the other couples, but I assume the success of their marriages follow the overall cultural trend. Whatever the outcome, it is a good thing that the stigma has been lifted and that people are free to live as they choose. Good marriages are about more than sex. The demystification of sex may be a good thing in the long run. There is simply not one way to live life, love another person, or be yourself.

A Word About Sex

The key to good sex is the key to all good faithful relationships: honest communication, respect, gentle care, and the honoring of the body, both yours and your partner's. Sex that dominates, demeans, and abuses, sex that is only about the needs and desires of one person, is not healthy.

The abundance of porn sites on the internet and the ease with which they can be found is especially dangerous for the young. Addiction is a real concern. The abuse and dehumanization of women is rampant. Many come to believe that what they see on the screen is how it should be in bed.

While the traditional church has offered more than its share of misinformation—leading with guilt and shame, beginning with blaming Eve for original sin and subsequently all women for leading men astray, cloistering and separating women and men, lifting up celibacy as the highest virtue, and making the false connection between sex and sinfulness—fundamentally Christianity celebrates the full expression of love, respect, tenderness, joy, and fun. The body is a temple to be honored and not abused. Therefore, we treat ourselves and others with deep respect. We express our affection in word and in deed, in touch, in listening, in caring, putting the needs of the other before our own. I think this is the way to be in intimate relationship with another. And, even though Jesus did not say anything about sex, I believe that his call for compassion, nonviolence, and love that puts the needs of other's first is a good guide to healthy intimate relationships.

In the years ahead and within the generations to follow, boundaries will be expanded, questions will be asked, choices will be made. Despite the backlash and the pendulum swing of culture, faithful curiosity, wonder, compassion, hospitality, and love will continue to show the way for those who love and live the questions.

CHAPTER 12

Do I Have to Believe in the Virgin Birth?

Creeds and Confessions

When [early Christians] recited their creeds they were not assenting to a set of propositions. The word *creedere*, for example, seems to have derived from *cor-dare*: to give one's heart. When they said "credo" this implied an emotional rather than an intellectual position.
—Karen Armstrong, *A History of God*

Someone who grew up in the Episcopal Church asked, "Do I have to believe the Nicene Creed?" I have had more than one person confess to me that when they are at church and a creed like the Apostles' or Nicene Creed is recited, they remain quiet. They don't want to recite something that they don't believe. Someone once shared with me that she crosses her fingers behind her back when she says the creed ("I'll say it, but I don't believe it!"). An Anglican priest once admitted that he can't say the creeds, so he sings them. I am not entirely sure I know what that means, but it seems to work for him. I have a friend who is a retired Episcopal priest who is uncomfortable attending the Episcopal service because each Sunday the Nicene Creed is said in the liturgy.

As a Presbyterian I am part of a denomination that places a great deal of emphasis on the church's creeds and confessions. Presbyterians have published a *Book of Confessions* that includes the Nicene Creed, completed in the late fourth century CE, and the "Brief Statement of Faith" published in 1983 at the reunion of the PCUS (the "southern" church) and the UPCUSA (the "northern" church).[1] The *Book of Confessions* also contains creeds and confessions from the sixteenth- and seventeenth-century Reformation period (the Scots Confession, the Heidelberg Catechism, the Second Helvetic Confession, the Westminster Standards); the "Theological Declaration of Barmen," written in 1934 in response to the rise of Adolph Hitler in Germany; the Confession of 1967, written by American Presbyterians in response to the social upheaval of those days; the Confession of Belhar, which arose out of the experience of twentieth-century South African apartheid; and the aforementioned "Brief Statement of Faith."

When pastors, elders, and deacons of the Presbyterian Church are brought before the congregation to be ordained and installed, they are asked this question: "Do you sincerely receive and adopt the essential tenets of the Reformed faith as expressed in the confessions of our church as authentic and reliable expositions of what Scripture leads us to believe and do, and will you be instructed and led by those confessions as you lead the people of God?"

If truth be told, most pastors, elders, and deacons know very little about the creeds and confessions. When I was asked by a committee evaluating my fitness to become a pastor what I thought of the Second Helvetic Confession, I responded, "Well, I like the First Helvetic Confession better." I had never read the second confession; in fact I had never heard of it, even though it is in the *Book of Confessions*. Thankfully my attempt at humor got a chuckle! By the way, the First Helvetic Confession didn't make the cut for the *Book of Confessions*, and I hadn't read it either!

---

1. Presbyterian Church (U.S.A.), *Book of Confessions*.

Do I Have to Believe in the Virgin Birth?

It is completely understandable when people respond negatively to the creeds and confessions or have questions. "Do I have to believe them?" "What does 'eternally begotten of the Father, God from God, Light from Light, true God from true God, begotten, not made, of one Being with the Father; through him all things were made' even mean?" "Do I have to believe in the Virgin Mary?" And, in the earliest creeds there is nothing about the life of Jesus, what he taught, or what he did. The Nicene Creed seems only interested that he was born, crucified, died, buried, and then rose on the third day.

Chapter 3 of the Scots Confession opens with these words: "By this transgression, generally known as original sin, the image of God was utterly defaced in man, and he and his children became by nature hostile to God, slaves to Satan, and servants to sin. And thus everlasting death has had, and shall have, power and dominion over all who have not been, are not, or shall not be reborn from above."[2] These are hardly encouraging words, especially for those drawn to the more joyful and communal aspects of Christian faith. They seem to emphasize the very beliefs that drive many seekers away from the church.

Many times, I have been asked, "John, you are a Presbyterian. Do you believe in predestination and that some people are destined for hell?" My answer is usually "no." However, back in the seventeenth century, the issue of whether God ordained some people to heaven and some to hell was a compelling and important theological issue, but thankfully not so much anymore. Now, the question is debated by historians and scholars of John Calvin.[3]

Some older Presbyterians remember when they were young and went through confirmation class. They had to study and recite parts of the Westminster Confession of Faith and its teaching manuals, the "catechism." The catechisms contained the questions and the answers of faith. I have always liked the first question and answer: "What is the chief end of man? Man's chief end is to glorify God, and

---

2. Presbyterian Church (U.S.A.), *Book of Confessions* 3.03.

3. John Calvin was the sixteenth-century Protestant Reformer who wrote *Institutes of the Christian Religion*.

What's Faith Got to Do With It?

to enjoy him forever."[4] I like a God that is to be enjoyed! However despite the first question, the formulaic structure and format, the preset questions and answers (as if we didn't have enough questions already), the masculine language, and the old-fashioned feel makes the catechism difficult to use and supports the negative feelings of those outside the community and even those within the church. Many respond, "I just don't believe it."

As one turns to the twentieth-century creeds, confessions, and declarations of faith, you notice a shift of emphasis and tone. At Barmen, representatives of the Lutheran, Reformed, and United Churches spoke with moral clarity against the rise of Hitler and his "German Christian" church. Of first and foremost importance was the confession that Jesus was Lord and the model for faithful living, not the führer.

The brave representatives, many of whom later were imprisoned, went into exile or hiding, or even executed, were collectively inspired to articulate a faith that was not based on pious words but rather motivated by faithful action. Grounded in their understanding of what the Bible teaches, these men (for they were all men) wrote a document that continues to inspire people of faith who are faced by tyrants and strong men who seek to usurp godlike status.

The Confession of 1967 broke with the traditional defining faith of the Westminster Confession of Faith to proclaim a new faith for a new age. America was going through the tumultuous era of civil rights, nuclear proliferation, the Vietnam War, and even rock and roll. Women were being liberated from the narrow expectations of post-war gender roles. The LGBTQA+ community was beginning to emerge and claim political power. Presbyterian Christians needed new words for a new social and historical context. Representatives gathered to see what the traditional faith still had to say. What came forth was an emphasis on "reconciliation" as the key scriptural concept.

The Belhar Confession arose from the political situation in South Africa. While some Christians used the Bible to support apartheid and the strict separation of the races, other Christians

---

4. Presbyterian Church (U.S.A.), *Book of Confessions* 7.001.

were rightly convinced that there was no such justification. Accepted by the Dutch Reformed Mission Church in 1986 and then adopted by the Presbyterian Church (U.S.A.) in 2004, the Belhar Confession proclaims with a moral force and theological clarity that the body of Christ should not be divided by narrow ideology. Like the Confession of 1967, Belhar stresses that the biblical concept of reconciliation is the fundamental message of Jesus; therefore, the work of the church is to dismantle systems and structures that failed to witness to this central message. The Belhar Confession rejected any doctrine "which absolutizes either natural diversity or the sinful separation of people," and therefore it rejects "any doctrine which, in such a situation, sanctions in the name of the gospel or of the will of God the forced separation of people on the grounds of race or color."[5]

The final confession (or creedal) statement in the Book of Confessions is "A Brief Statement of Faith." Beginning with words that recall the language of the earliest creeds, the statement declares, following the Confession of 1967 and Belhar, that God is calling believers into a new age where everyone is equally made in God's image. To deny or dismiss anyone as a beloved child of God is rebelling against what God intends. One cannot "exploit neighbor and nature." The role of the believer is to have courage to "unmask idolatries in Church and culture, to hear the voices of people long silenced, and to work with others for justice, freedom and peace."[6]

Certainly, I am drawn to the confessions of the twentieth and twenty-first centuries. I give my heart to the statements that seek to speak a new word to this age and to include all people regardless of race, gender, or identity. These later confessions and statements use language I understand and speak to a world that I live in. The emphasis is not on doctrinal certainty but in living with compassion, forgiveness, inclusion, and justice. The older confessions and creeds, not so much. However, giving them their due, the older creeds and confessions are attempts to articulate faith in their historical and cultural context.

5. Presbyterian Church (U.S.A.), *Book of Confessions* 10.4, 10.6.
6. Presbyterian Church (U.S.A.), *Book of Confessions* 11.3, 11.4.

The Nicene and Apostles' Creeds were formulated in the first centuries of the church when people were asking, "What do we believe?" and "What are the essential beliefs of Christianity?" It was the same question that Jill asked me in the 1980s!

The Reformation documents were formulated at a time of disruption: Protestants and Catholics split after sixteen hundred years of there being only one dominant church. Those who broke off from Catholicism needed new statements that articulated new beliefs and defined what made the new expression different from the old. The reformation of the church was happening concurrently with the social and political disruption of the age. The twentieth- and twenty-first-century faith statements, like the eras before them, were asking new questions of the old tradition and coming up with new answers.

The *Book of Confession* doesn't demand conformity. Rather, the collection of creeds and confessions is living proof that questions drive faith. Occasionally, throughout history, people have gathered to ask their questions of the old traditions seeking new answers for a new day. The *Book of Confessions* serves as a model for this book you are reading. Gathering in small groups, people seek a new vocabulary for the real life they live. Old formulations are honored but replaced. The essentials are refined and given new meaning. Those who are adamant that you must believe "this or that" and remain stuck in the language of the old creeds are missing the whole point of them.

So no, you don't have to use the language of the Nicene Creed. You don't have to believe in the same way that Christians believed in the sixteenth century. Curious and inquisitive people continue to ask their questions and to reform and refine the faith of the past. But it is good to recognize that these earlier Christians were doing the same thing that we are doing today—loving and living the questions, leading with curiosity to seek to understand what is going on.

As your faith seeks understanding, if the Nicene Creed works for you, go with it! If not, perhaps one of the more modern statements resonate with you. However, it may be that it is time to gather to rewrite and rethink and continue the journey!

Chapter 13

What Do I Have to Believe?
Conclusion

We shall cease from exploration and the end of all our exploring will be to arrive where we started and know the place for the first time.

—T. S. Eliot, "Little Gidding"

James Joyce, in a blessed moment of succinctness, had it right when asked to define Catholicism: "Here comes everybody." That's a notion also found in *The Diary of a Country Priest* by George Bernanos: "We've got to make room for everything and everybody—goats included. Whether it be a goat or a lambkin, the Master expects each beast to be returned in a healthy condition." While some in the flock bleat and others baa, everyone—senator, cardinals, preachers of virtue and dispensers of mayhem—have a place in the choir. Exclude any of them and you have a club, not a church.

—Coleman McCarthy, *Washington Post*, October 17, 1994

My wife and I have been watching the television series *Somebody, Somewhere*.[1] The show is set in Manhattan, Kansas. It is about

---

1. Duplass, "BFD."

finding friends and belonging to a community. It is also about faith and church, although these themes are a bit more understated. As the series unfolds, an odd collection of misfits in their forties dealing with past grief, choices, and identities find each other. It is one of the most refreshing and moving televisions shows we have seen in a long time.

In one episode Joel, played by Jeff Hiller, strikes up a friendship with a coworker, Sam, played by Bridget Everett. Sam is dealing with the grief of losing her sister to cancer. Joel, who is gay and was bullied in high school, now attends the local Presbyterian church on Sundays. He likes it. In fact, he wonders if he has a calling to be a minister.

However, Joel's heart is at "choir practice." In an empty mall store one evening a week, an open mic is set up and drinks and snacks are served. Fred Rococco, played by the gender-bending comedian Murray Hill, is a kind of pastor figure, serving as a master of ceremonies. One evening Joel invites Sam to this "choir practice" congregation. He encourages Sam to sing for the assembled crowd. Sam, a gifted singer, hasn't performed since her high school days more than twenty years before. Sam steps forward. Hesitant at first, Sam finds her spirit and voice and lets it all go, singing "A Piece of My Heart," made famous by Janis Joplin in the 1960s.

Sam's spirit and energy pulls everyone together. She gives a piece of her heart to the crowd. One person in the audience leans to the person next to him and says, "Now this is church!" Not the sermon, not the hymns, not the anthem—but the community of seekers, questioners, and doubters, drawn together as they seek to belong to each other. The old church, the old ways, no longer fulfilling. New forms shaped by questions being answered in new ways. I think "choir practice" may be closer to the original first church. It's about hospitality, curiosity, being together, sharing food, and celebrating the gifts of those assembled. "This is church!" Amen.

From my experiences, I have learned that people want to feel connected to others, to give their hearts and imaginations to something larger than themselves, to sense some meaning in our world that flows underneath the day-to-day craziness. No one wants to feel judged by what they don't know or don't understand, who they are, what they are confident about, and what they doubt. Deep in all of us is a longing for community; in short, we want to belong to something, to belong to ourselves and to others, shaped by our highest aspirations. Only by building safe and open communities, inviting people to get connected without fear of judgment, will people feel safe to grow into whatever faith they want to live by.

In fact, if the Christian church has a future, I think it needs to reclaim what it was at the beginning, and that is to be a community first and foremost of belonging, welcoming everyone. Treat everyone with respect. If nothing else, live the Golden Rule: do unto others as you would have them do unto you. In other words, behave in a way that builds community. As your sense of belonging deepens, and your behavior is shaped by hospitality and service, you will find words for your thoughts. You will begin to name your feelings, hopes, and aspirations. In short, you will come to believe *something*—and on you go!

For faith, belief, trust-shaped imagination is not a once in a lifetime profession fully conceived and expressed. Rather faith changes, matures, and fills out. Sometimes it is important to throw everything out and start again by asking the most basic questions and sharing them in community. Faith is formed and found in community with others.

When we are hesitant to ask our questions, share our doubts, and express our yearnings of the moment, we extinguish the flame of community and self-expression; we limit ourselves and narrow our scope, afraid that we might say something that is not acceptable.

But in our yearning to put words to that which our hearts long for, we have to be vulnerable and love our questions and live our questions until greater clarity comes.

In the eleventh century BCE, Anselm of Canterbury was the first to use the phrase *fides quaerens intellectum* ("faith seeking understanding"). Faith is always a matter of seeking after, of bumping into, moments of clarity and at times falling into shadow and uncertainty, of taking the next step into the ray of light that is before you, trusting that the source of light is "out there!"

What's Faith Got to Do With It?

I believe that truth always points beyond itself. Anything we come up with is, at best, approximations. The very nature of language both limits and liberates us: Limits us because we don't get the words right. Liberates us because we get to try and try again.

Learn to be comfortable with not having to know. I have always appreciated the story of the man whose wife died unexpectedly just when the couple, who had been married for many years, was retiring and planning trips around the world. The widower was devastated. He would walk miles asking God *why*. "Why did you let my wife die?" Day after day, week after week, month after month, the man walked and asked this question. One morning, crossing the field, the man sensed an "inner voice" not heard but intuited. It was an answer to his question of why. The answer was, "You don't need to know." The man found this experience liberating. Still missing his wife and the love of his life, he found a way to move on living more fully, being open to whatever came next. The answers may be different for you, but keep asking until you too sense a new answer and a new direction.

So, love and live your questions. Be open to changing your mind if the facts challenge you or your circumstances cause you see things in a new light. Start with what you *do* affirm, what you *do* give your heart to. Don't give more power to your doubt than to your curiosity. Maintain your healthy skepticism, but don't give in to your cynicism. Celebrate your doubt as the starting point! As Frederick Buechner wrote, "Whether your faith is that there is a God or that there is not a God, if you don't have any doubts, you are either kidding yourself or asleep. Doubts are the ants in the pants of faith. They keep it awake and moving."[2]

Of great importance is to practice what you believe currently. Ask yourself, "How do I interpret what is going on in the world right now?" As shared earlier in this book, if you believe that we are all going to "hell in a handbasket," this will shape your living. However, if you think that a power of goodness permeates creation, then focus on that. You can change your mind and actions as you go along! Get out of your head and step out.

---

2. "Doubt," in Buechner, *Wishful Thinking*, 23.

What Do I Have to Believe?

As you are creating your life, you will get messy, you will make mistakes. As Eugene Peterson wrote, "Creativity is not neat. It is not orderly. When we are being creative a great deal of what we do is wrong. When we are being creative, we are not efficient."[3] So, learn to love your mess, keep working with it. Continue to move along the path of discovery. As my mentor Rev. Herb Meza used to say, "Faith is found, not on location but in locomotion."

I now am ready to answer that question that Jill first asked me. "What do I have to believe to be a Christian?" My answer is, *nothing*. You don't *have* to believe anything dogmatic or doctrinal. However, if you are drawn to the challenge of following the way, the truth, and the life of Jesus, which is, as described in an earlier chapter, a way of compassion, mercy, nonviolence, hospitality, and self-sacrifice for the good of others, then claim the name; the details of belief will come in the living.

Live the question, honor your life and the lives of others, and you will bump into signposts that will point the way. In time you may be able to put words to your longing and have answers for your questions. But I am more interested in what you do and how you live than what you believe. Christianity is a faith tradition that invites you to "come and see" (John 1:39), to explore the fullness of life, and to be welcomed into a large community of fellow seekers.

In the days ahead, as you are coming up with your questions and learning to love them, do the following:

Start praying. Set aside time for reflection and see what happens. Perhaps begin a journal and keep track of what you are experiencing.

Read one of the Gospels and see where that leads you. Mark passages that catch your attention with a highlighter so you can come back to them. Jot down your questions.

Pay attention to where your money goes. Do your "Venmos" reflect your deepest values? I have heard it said that your checkbook is a moral document. There is truth in that.

---

3. Peterson, *Under the Unpredictable Plant*, 184.

Are you involved in some form of advocacy work? Get involved in some volunteer activity with, for example, a local food bank or homeless shelter. Call your elected officials and let them know how you feel about issues that matter to you.

Find a community of friends and form a "Living the Question" study group. Share your questions. What does following the way, the truth, and the life of Jesus mean to you? How might that point the way forward?

If you are not ready to call yourself a "Christian," don't worry about it. Today that term is so loaded. Back in the first days of the church, the followers of Jesus called themselves part of the "way." They called each other brother and sister. Today we might call each other siblings. The first church was a new kind of family that was identified not by DNA but by mutual concern. The early church gathered in homes, read and discussed the Bible, shared a meal, and remembered Jesus by breaking the bread and sharing the cup. They then moved outside the home into the world, spreading the good news in word and, more importantly, in deed that everyone was a beloved child of God, worthy, precious, gifted, included, forgiven, and free. It wasn't a transaction (believe this or else), it was a proclamation. It wasn't about doctrine or dogma.

One of my favorite stories of the early church is from the early Christian writer Tertullian. He describes a community that was being ravaged by the plague. People were fleeing their homes. Of course, the plague was spread as they moved from town to town! However, there is a note written by one of these fleeing Roman citizens. He notices that the Christian community is staying and taking care of each other and whoever comes to them. The writer is amazed and writes, "See how they love each other."[4] May this be the description that people make about the new community of seekers who love and live the questions. Perhaps there is a future for the church after all.

---

4. See Tertullian, *Apology* 39.

Selected Bibliography

Appian. *Roman History, Vol. III, The Civil Wars, Books 1–3.26* (Loeb Classical Library No. 4). Harvard University Press, Cambridge. 1913.

Armstrong, Karen. *A History of God: The 4,000-Year Quest of Judaism, Christianity and Islam.* New York: Ballantine, 1993.

Aslan, Reza. *Zealot: The Life and Times of Jesus of Nazareth.* New York: Random House, 2013.

Barton, John. *How the Bible Came to Be.* Louisville: Westminster John Knox, 1998.

Bauer, Walter, et al. *Greek-English Lexicon of the New Testament and Other Early Christian Literature.* 2nd ed. Chicago: University of Chicago Press, 1979.

Beal, Timothy. *The Rise and Fall of the Bible: The Unexpected History of an Accidental Book.* Boston: Houghton Mifflin Harcourt, 2011.

Bell, Rob. *Love Wins: A Book About Heaven, Hell, and the Fate of Every Person Who Ever Lived.* New York: HarperOne, 2012.

Bolz-Weber, Nadia. *Accidental Saints: Finding God in All the Wrong People.* New York: Convergent, 2015.

Borg, Marcus. *The Heart of Christianity: Rediscovering a Life of Faith.* New York: HarperCollins, 2003.

Brooks, Garth. "Unanswered Prayers." Track 7 on *No Fences.* Capitol Nashville, 1990.

Brown, Francis, et al. *A Hebrew and English Lexicon of the Old Testament.* Oxford: Clarendon, 1978.

Brueggemann, Walter. *The Message of the Psalms: A Theological Commentary.* Minneapolis: Fortress, 1985.

———. *The Prophetic Imagination.* 40th anniv. ed. Minneapolis: Fortress, 2018.

Buechner, Frederick. *Wishful Thinking: A Seeker's ABC.* San Francisco: Harper, 1973.

Burns, Robert. "A Red, Red Rose." 1794. Poetry by Heart. https://www.poetrybyheart.org.uk/poems/a-red-red-rose.

Butler, Octavia. *The Parable of the Sower.* New York: Grand Central, 1993.

Selected Bibliography

Carroll, James. *Constantine's Sword: The Church and the Jews; A History.* Boston: Houghton Mifflin, 2002.
Cather, Willa. *My Ántonia.* Boston: Mariner Classics, 1995.
Church of the Saviour. "Origins." Inward/Outward Together. https://inwardoutward.org/origins/.
Conzelmann, Hans. *The Theology of St. Luke.* Translated by Geoffrey Buswell. London: Faber, 1960.
Cosby, N. Gordon. *By Grace Transformed: Christianity for a New Millennium.* New York: Crossroads, 1999.
Crossan, John D. *The Birth of Christianity.* San Francisco: HarperOne, 1998.
———. *God and Empire: Jesus Against Rome, Then and Now.* New York: HarperOne, 2007.
———. *The Historical Jesus: The Life of a Mediterranean Jewish Peasant.* San Francisco: HarperSanFrancisco, 2008.
———. *How to Read the Bible and Still Be a Christian: Is God Violent? An Exploration from Genesis to Revelation.* New York: HarperOne, 2016.
Dalai Lama. *Freedom in Exile: The Autobiography of the Dalai Lama.* New York: HarperCollins, 1990.
Dawkins, Richard. *The God Delusion.* London: Bantam, 2006.
Dickinson, Emily. *The Complete Poems of Emily Dickinson.* Edited by Thomas H. Johnson. London: Faber & Faber, 2016.
Douglas-Klotz, Neil. *Prayers of the Cosmos: Meditations on the Aramaic Words of Jesus.* New York: HarperOne, 2009.
Duplass, Jay. "BFD." *Somebody, Somewhere*, season 1, episode 1. HBO, aired Jan. 16, 2022.
Fawcett, John. "Blest Be the Tie That Binds." Hymnary.org. https://hymnary.org/text/blest_be_the_tie_that_binds.
Graham, Ruth. "He Gave a Name to What Many Christians Feel." *New York Times*, Mar. 10, 2025. https://www.nytimes.com/2025/03/06/us/aaron-renn-christianity-conservative-negative-world.html.
Greyson, Bruce. *After: A Doctor Explores What Near-Death Experiences Reveal About Life and Beyond.* New York: St. Martin's, 2021.
Guiora, Amos. *Armies of Enablers: Survivor Stories of Complicity and Betrayal in Sexual Assaults.* Chicago: American Bar Association, 2020.
Heschel, Abraham Joshua. *God in Search of Man: A Philosophy of Judaism.* New York: Farrar, Straus & Giroux, 1955.
———. *Man's Quest for God.* Santa Fe, NM: Aurora, 1998.
Jagger, Mick, and Keith Richards. "You Can't Always Get What You Want." Track 5 on *Let it Bleed.* London Records, 1969.
Josephus. *Jewish Antiquities, Volume VIII: Books 18–19.* Translated by Louis H. Feldman. Loeb Classical Library 433. Cambridge: Harvard University Press, 1965.
Keating, Thomas. *Open Mind, Open Heart.* New York: Bloomsbury, 1994.
Keller, Helen. *Open Door.* New York: Doubleday, 1957.

Selected Bibliography

Kristol, Irving. "Christmas, Christians, and Jews." *National Review*, Dec. 30, 1988. https://www.nationalreview.com/1988/12/christmas-christians-and-jews/.
Lamott, Anne. *Help, Thanks, Wow: The Three Essential Prayers*. New York: Penguin, 2012.
Lentz, John C., Jr. "Living the Question: What Good Is Prayer?" Substack, Oct. 28, 2024. https://johnlentz.substack.com/p/living-the-question-4c5.
———. *Luke's Portrait of Paul*. Society for New Testament Studies Monograph Series 77. Cambridge: Cambridge University Press, 1993.
Levine, Amy-Jill. *Short Stories by Jesus: The Enigmatic Parables of a Controversial Rabbi*. Nashville: Abingdon, 2014.
Lewis, C. S. *Mere Christianity*. New York: Simon & Schuster, 1980.
Manning, Brennan. *The Ragamuffin Gospel: Embracing the Unconditional Love of God*. Colorado Springs, CO: Multnomah, 1990.
Marks, Julia. "Sermon: Alex's Death, by William Sloane Coffin, Jr." Transcript, Value of Sparrows, Oct. 6, 2013. https://thevalueofsparrows.wordpress.com/2013/10/06/sermon-alexs-death-by-william-sloane-coffin-jr/.
Marshall, Bruce. *All Glorious Within*. London: Constable, 1944.
Martel, Yann. *Life of Pi*. New York: Harcourt, 2001.
Mattison, Mark M., trans. *The Infancy Gospel of Thomas*. https://www.gospels.net/infancythomas.
Merton, Thomas. *Thoughts on Solitude*. New York: Farrar, Straus & Giroux, 1956.
Moore, Russell. "President Trump: Now What for the Church?" Russell Moore (website), Nov. 9, 2016. https://www.russellmoore.com/2016/11/09/president-trump-now-church/.
Nguyen, Bao, dir. *The Greatest Night in Pop*. Los Gatos, CA: Netflix, 2024.
Nhất Hạnh, Thích. *Loving Buddha, Loving Christ*. New York: Penguin, 1995.
Norris, Kathleen. *Dakota: A Spiritual Geography*. New York: HarperOne, 2001.
O'Connor, Flannery. *The Complete Stories*. New York: Farrar, Straus & Giroux, 1971.
Osborne, Joan. "One of Us." Written by Eric Bazilian. Track 6 on *Relish*. Mercury Records, 1995.
Pagels, Elaine. *Beyond Belief: The Secret Gospel of Thomas*. New York: Random House, 2005.
———. *Miracles and Wonder: The Historical Mystery of Jesus*. New York: Random House, 2025.
Peterson, Eugene. *Under the Unpredictable Plant: An Exploration in Vocational Holiness*. Grand Rapids: Eerdmans, 1992.
Presbyterian Church (U.S.A.). *Book of Confessions Study Edition*. Rev. ed. Louisville: Westminster John Knox, 2017.
Prine, John. "Jesus: The Missing Years." Track 14 on *The Missing Years*. Oh Boy Records, 1991
Rauch, Jonathan. *Cross Purposes: Christianity's Broken Bargain with Democracy*. New Haven: Yale University Press, 2025.

Selected Bibliography

Remen, Rachel Naomi. *Kitchen Table Wisdom: Stories That Heal.* New York: Penguin, 2006.

Renn, Aaron M. *Life in the Negative World: Confronting Challenges in an Anti-Christian Culture.* Grand Rapids: Zondervan, 2024.

Rowling, J. K. *Harry Potter and the Deathly Hallows.* Hoboken, NJ: Arthur A. Levine, 2007.

Shelley, Percy Bysshe. *Prometheus Unbound.* Edited by Vida D. Scudder. Boston: D. C. Heath, 1892.

Smith, Gregory A., et al. "Religious Landscape Study: Executive Summary." Pew Research Center, Feb. 26, 2025. https://www.pewresearch.org/religion/2025/02/26/religious-landscape-study-executive-summary/.

Smith, Huston. *The Soul of Christianity: Restoring the Great Tradition.* New York: HarperOne, 2006.

Spielberg, Steven, dir. *Raiders of the Lost Ark.* Los Angeles: Paramount, 1981.

Spong, John Shelby. *Why Christianity Must Change or Die: A Bishop Speaks to Believers in Exile.* New York: HarperOne, 1999.

Steinbeck, John. *East of Eden.* New York: Penguin, 1952.

Stone, Roxanne, and Katelyn Beaty. "Blowing Up the Evangelical Bro Code." *Saved by the City*, podcast audio, 42 min. Religion News Service, Mar. 7, 2024. https://religionnews.com/2024/03/07/blowing-up-the-evangelical-bro-code/.

Suetonius. *Lives of the Caesars, Volume I: Julius. Augustus. Tiberius. Gaius Caligula.* Translated by J. C. Rolfe. Introduction by K. R. Bradley. Loeb Classical Library 31. Cambridge: Harvard University Press, 1914.

Talbott, Harold. *Tendrel: A Memoir of New York and the Buddhist Himalayas.* Marion, MA: Buddhayana Foundation, 2019.

Tertullian. *Apology: De Spectaculis.* Translated by T. R. Glover. Loeb Classical Library 250. Cambridge: Harvard University Press, 1931.

Tolkien, J. R. R. *The Fellowship of the Ring.* Boston: Houghton Mifflin, 1965.

Tutu, Desmond. *An African Prayer Book.* New York: Image, 1995.

Untermeyer, Louis, ed. *Modern American Poetry.* Rev. ed. New York: Harcourt, Brace, 1921. https://www.gutenberg.org/cache/epub/58992/pg58992-images.html.

Walker, Alice. *Anything We Love Can Be Saved: A Writer's Activism.* New York: Ballantine, 1997.

Wallis, James. *God's Politics: Why the Right Gets It Wrong and the Left Doesn't Get It.* San Francisco: Harper, 2005.

Weems, Ann. "I No Longer Pray for Peace." The Well, InterVarsity Women Scholars and Professionals, Mar. 10, 2022. https://thewell.intervarsity.org/arts-books-and-media/i-no-longer-pray-peace.html.

www.ingramcontent.com/pod-product-compliance
Lightning Source LLC
Chambersburg PA
CBHW072146160426
43197CB00012B/2266